Marco Previero discovered writing late in life, after his daughter Millie was diagnosed with brain cancer in 2013. Since then, he has published a book, national articles and appeared both on TV and radio programmes to advocate for better quality of life for childhood brain tumour survivors. When he is not writing, Marco spends his time both as a Trustee of Success Life After Cure Ltd, the charity this book is in support of, and running his business. He lives in London with his wife and his three children and spends much of his free time dreaming of a cure for the many life-altering late side effects childhood brain tumours often bring.

Dr Helen Spoudeas qualified in 1981 from Barts Hospital, London, later obtained Paediatric Specialisation in 1985, and finally attained her postgraduate doctorate (MD) in 1995. She is a fellow of the Royal College of Physicians (FRCP) and of Child Health (FRCPCH). In 1999, she became a consultant paediatric endocrinologist at University College Hospital and Great Ormond Street Hospitals, a post she semi-retired from in 2020. Since then, she has led the launch of Success Life After Cure Limited, a national charity whose aim is to enable better futures for survivors of childhood brain tumours.

Success Life After Cure Ltd charity exists to raise
awareness of, and support life-changing growth,
developmental, neuroendocrine and mental health
effects, of a brain tumour in childhood during and
beyond cure.

www.successcharity.org.uk
Registered Charity Number: 1188298

WALKING
ON
THE EDGE

*Thoughts on life and parenting after
childhood brain cancer*

Marco Previero

Matador
Unit E2 Airfield Business Park,
Harrison Road, Market Harborough,
Leicestershire. LE16 7UL
Tel: 0116 2792299
Email: books@troubador.co.uk
Web: www.troubador.co.uk/matador
Twitter: @matadorbooks

ISBN 978 1803131 771

British Library Cataloguing in Publication Data.
A catalogue record for this book is available from the British Library.

Printed and bound in the UK by TJ Books LTD, Padstow, Cornwal
Typeset in 11pt Minion Pro by Troubador Publishing Ltd, Leicester, UK

Matador is an imprint of Troubador Publishing Ltd

To Vanessa, Ellie, Millie, and Luca

CONTENTS

Themes: Coping with traumatic events. Dealing with uncertainty. Paediatric brain cancers: what are they exactly? Why do they happen? The nature of choice when children are involved. Talking to children about cancer.

Themes: Dealing with a shattered future. Children's outlook during and after treatment. Being newbies. How children cope with therapy. How to cope with this total disease. Feeling helpless. Telling children the truth. Understanding chemotherapy. Evaluating long-term side effects.

Themes: How siblings cope with a cancer diagnosis. Talking to siblings about cancer. Contemplating the loss of a child.

Chemotherapy: the good, the bad and the ugly. Chemo's side effects. The kindness of strangers. Ways to think about the future. The truth about "progression-free survival".

Themes: Post-traumatic stress for children and parents. The vocabulary of cancer. Reframing how we think about this disease. Coping with the long-term side effects of cancer. What are they and how can they be managed? Dealing with grief.

FOREWORD

By Dr Helen Spoudeas MBBS DRCOG FRCP FRCPCH MD, Paediatric & Adolescent Endocrinologist & Chair of Success Life After Cure Ltd

Cure Alone Is Not Enough

Surviving a childhood brain tumour

Surviving brain cancer or any brain tumour in childhood is just the first hard-won step on a life-long journey which, on average, can span over sixty years. It is hardest for those children surviving multiple, toxic, high-dose and transplant therapies, head or whole-spine irradiation, metastatic or second cancers and, importantly, unpredicted brain injury arising from tumour location as well as treatment. Much of the quality of survival research collected over the last twenty years shows that, if we do nothing, there is an inexorable decline in cognitive, emotional and mental health well-being over the growing years. It tends to be worst for those that are infants and generally under seven years of age at diagnosis and who, therefore, have the greatest developmental journey ahead. They face the longest opportunity to "fall" before they meet criteria for helpful intervention. Conversely, they also possess the greatest ability to adapt and benefit from rehabilitation to reach their own potential, whilst they are still maturing. They often have the smallest voice to request our help.

Investment in cancer research and intensified treatments now means some eighty per cent of children with a brain tumour live at least five years after diagnosis. But while ever-younger children and even new-born infants, tolerate (much better than adults) increasingly burdensome and repeated experimental therapies, it's easy to forget the "cure's" heavy price on the developing child. This is especially true for paradoxically "benign" tumours with malign positions close to the brain's deep, primitive, midbrain control centre, vital for life itself.

Some two-thirds of survivors experience more than one (many up to five or six) significant, long-term, sensory, neurological or life-threatening disabilities such as vision, hearing, speech and language impairment, learning and behavioural difficulties. They often feel socially alienated and unable to thrive. Without ongoing support, these children can struggle to achieve their growth potential, reach adolescence and sexual maturity, complete their schooling and develop meaningful peer relationships. Later on, this can impact on their ability to live full, independent adult lives. Others will need to access educational, neurocognitive, or clinical psychology services but also psychiatric support for behavioural issues, low mood and other mental health disorders.

For most, vital rehabilitative lifelines remain unobtainable; developmental gaps and opportunities for support are missed, as symptoms evolve over many maturing years. Mental health and schooling issues are often unmasked too late, during the peak period of adolescent brain maturation at secondary or further education; youngsters can experience victimisation, fatigue, examination failures and vocational discrimination, or maladjustment to secondary, chronic health problems (heart, kidney, gut/enteral, hormonal), which can themselves be life-threatening. An unlucky few will never truly be rid of their brain tumour and receive continuous repeated cycles of experimental treatments. Others will be tripped unexpectedly in young adulthood by a second primary tumour elsewhere or a second acute brain injury from a mechanical (e.g. shunt) malfunction, brain infection or haemorrhage/bleed. And yet, all too often this new and growing community of survivors can find it difficult to access just as vital, neurodevelopmental, vocational and mental health NHS services during and beyond the neuro-oncology treatment itself. This can be especially true for a vital minority who are most brain injured, least able to speak for themselves and without a parental advocate.

The consequences of growing with and surviving a childhood brain tumour are often not prioritised within our "cancer-directed" healthcare setting. Existing neuro-oncology and so-called "cancer late effects" services do not always provide fully for this group's individualised, complex, and "invisible" needs. By definition this group starts with an unrecognised and uncharacterised acquired brain injury that varies by tumour position (deep midbrain or peripheral), is not alleviated by cure and is aggravated by disease relapse and treatment failures. We don't yet know which early, intensive and ongoing rehabilitation works best for them. Surely, they deserve just as much investment in proactive rehabilitative research from the beginning and throughout their growing years, as a mandated parallel part of their "cure" pathway?

The importance of early parallel brain injury assessments and neurorehabilitation

Getting a neurodevelopmental assessment from the beginning and at each (of a potential four) key maturational stages, can make such a difference to helping children achieve their potential and to preventing them deviating too far from it. But unlike tumour treatment pathways, parallel brain injury assessment and support services are patchy and limited, administered too late, temporarily funded (by charities or research grants) and unavailable to every child from diagnosis to maturity. All too often, these same individuals who have struggled so hard to survive early childhood, and to maintain their developmental trajectory, must in mid-childhood, adolescence or young adulthood, be allowed to fail, to fall to a level where their needs become acute and where they are most likely to suffer long-term harm, before they meet criteria for educational, vocational, mental health or neuro-disability support.

In addition, already stretched community health, education and social care may deem their multiple health and life-threatening hormone needs too complex and too chronic for local child development or acquired brain injury services, or for adult traumatic brain injury rehabilitation. The increasing subspecialisation of medical provision to support the consequences of such rare disease puts additional pressure on survivors to seek out, and allocate the time to benefit from, appropriate ongoing rehabilitative interventions. Moreover, more can be done to ensure such specialist medical care, in this new complex field, is delivered in a more holistic fashion, and any lessons learnt disseminated to the community educational establishments and employers. This field, which must compete with already stretched NHS resources to undertake neuroscience and neuroendocrine research into these injuries at the same time as the investigations of "heroic" new brain tumour cures, is hard to fund, develop and deliver. All of which, in turn, renders them inaccessible to many and increases the vital "cost" of a cure in childhood.

Cure alone is not enough – Success Life After Cure Ltd

For survivors of childhood brain tumours, cure alone is no longer enough. The time has come to forcefully advocate for a switch from increasing cure rates to improving the quality of survival for those injured by their disease and its toxic therapy. Every child treated for a brain tumour, regardless of its grade or treatment modality, and especially those in the vital deep midbrain, deserves a parallel separate neuroendocrine and rehabilitative treatment pathway which includes a comprehensive basal assessment to inform future education and care. This can then be updated and revised at key stages towards adult transition.

With this mission in mind Success Life After Cure Ltd, a charity whose objective is to enable brighter futures for childhood brain tumour survivors, was born. It was in its infancy just before I semi-retired from Great Ormond Street

Hospital and University College Hospital as lead consultant endocrinologist to the paediatric oncology service two years ago, but it really began some twenty years ago. Back then, there was a lower survival base and little understanding that a brain tumour cure differed from that of other childhood cancers in causing a significant, inevitable and unaddressed brain injury whose cause (or set of causes) had probably less to do with brain irradiation and more to do with tumour position and its developmental consequences for which children need and deserve support.

Raising funds and public awareness to support gaps in neurorehabilitation for this "brain tumour survivor cohort" has always been a low priority for the NHS nationwide and, despite my efforts, also at my own, largest and highly regarded 'beacon' service. But with high cure rates, holistic neuroendocrine and rehabilitative services which were not foreseen, are now vital and increasingly mandated. While research and service funding continue into ongoing cures, and support to maintain growth and to balance other hormonal deficiencies (well-established treatments which, if timely, produce excellent outcomes), these children also need more investment and research to support their innate intellectual trajectory and emotional well-being.

I have felt compelled to continue advocating for parallel neurodevelopmental assessments to inform therapeutic, mental health and educational interventions for every child with a brain tumour. This is important, not just for those undergoing research assessments, nor for the most damaged or disabled, but for every child's innate potential as they navigate four key developmental stages to mature adulthood, after which it may be too late. We know from cases of traumatic brain injury and from assessing medical injury and negligence claims of tumour-induced brain injuries, that intensive, early and ongoing neurorehabilitation, while very costly, can also be "game-changing". Our aims have government backing, willing donors and plenty of government and professional guidelines against which they should have been fully implemented into commissioned services. But such services are not always part of routine NHS "pathway"-led referral criteria and of low priority to charities advocating for research into cure or to NHS England or other research funding. They remain, generally, difficult to access and patchy compared with services for the cure itself, despite government[1] guidance on neuro-rehabilitation provision and funding for two new national proton beam centres and additional paediatric professional endorsement for improving outcomes from childhood stroke and rare endocrine tumours[2].

It is also becoming clear to me that the devastating midbrain (hypothalamic) injury now seen, results from the position (rather than the grade and hence treatment) of these so-called "benign" tumours with which many, particularly young, children struggle. For many survivors and their families, it casts a dark shadow over brain tumour cure and requires dedicated neuroendocrine and neuro-oncology collaborative services. This and other potentially remediable and mislabelled "late treatment effects", actually begin with the tumour and evolve from diagnosis. It is timely to improve the way in which we address them so that children can fulfil their true potential, achieve independence and, as adults, seek employment. Only then can we truly claim their cure as a success.

As a charity, our board are absolutely committed to supporting and interconnecting all childhood brain tumour survivors of any age, nationwide, helping the NHS bridge service gaps with novel therapies such as digital telerehabilitation services, developing (paediatric neuro-oncology) centre rehabilitative expertise, community health and education liaison, expert and peer to peer advocacy as well as assessment at the four key neurodevelopmental stages which enable a child to contemplate a brighter future after surviving a childhood brain tumour.

Millie Previero – walking on the edge
One such child is Millie Previero. Millie was referred to Great Ormond Street Hospital (GOSH) on 6 April 2013, when she was seven years old, as an emergency. She complained of decreased vision over the previous two days. An MRI scan had revealed a possible midbrain tumour above the vital pituitary gland which was pressurising her optic nerves and threatening her sight. Following an urgent visual assessment at Moorfield's Eye Hospital, she was admitted to GOSH for further care.

The story you are about to read is engrossing, honest and ultimately life-affirming without offering a flat "happily ever after" conclusion. Marco handles the subject matter, and the deep conflicting emotions it engenders, with thoughtful insight and confidence. The latter is borne out of a deeply felt and researched meditation on the experience of a father whose young child is suddenly diagnosed with a rare brain cancer. This book is a self-exploration, a narrative of how a beloved daughter's life-threatening illness and need for recurrent surgery and prolonged toxic therapy to her young, maturing and innocent brain – her very being – irrevocably altered his own view of the world and his sense of self. It also undoubtedly changed the future developmental trajectory and life opportunities of his child and impacted his wider family. The book's pages are well-balanced between the emotional rollercoaster of such a painful experience and the strength derived from Marco and his wife Vanessa's partnership, their concerted efforts to be a step ahead in understanding, and thereby limiting the risks, medical complications, and long-term consequences of, Millie's disease and its draconian cure.

I have never ceased to be in awe of children's resilience and have long recognised their insuperable capacity to heal not just themselves but others, especially their parents. Marco's reflections are aided by Millie's own remarkable insights, revealed during their intimate forest walks, over many growing years and long after treatment has ended. These insights are extraordinary, provocative, and illuminating to those of us, including health professionals, who experience such circumstances "second-hand". They help explain why I am committed to supporting this aftermath.

However, these experiences must be very familiar, perhaps even ordinary, to other parents like Marco and Vanessa Previero and to other children like Millie who courageously undergo similar treatment for brain tumours, whether benign or malignant, and emerge to tell their tale.

I am indebted to Marco for sharing his hard-earnt wisdom, for donating his book's proceeds to our cause and for his tireless commitment as a founding trustee of the charity. I believe you too will find his story fascinating and thought-provoking, by turns harrowing, moving and lyrical.

Finally, dear reader, I am grateful to you for also supporting our vision. Net proceeds of this book will fund projects identified as critical by Success Life After Cure Ltd, to help every child regain their future. For this, I and my trustees extend our heartfelt thanks.

Helen Spoudeas, London, January 2022

A BRIEF NOTE TO THE READER

Back in 2013, my daughter Millie, then aged seven, was diagnosed with a rare form of malignant brain tumour. She was treated at Great Ormond Street Hospital and whilst she has been "cured" of cancer, she lives with severe, life-altering disabilities as a result of her illness and its related treatment. Nothing can prepare you for those life-changing events, but I felt at the time that not enough relevant, factual storytelling material was available to parents when this happens. This is the book I needed, as a parent and carer, when Millie was first diagnosed. It aims to provide insights on the many challenges parents face during and after treatment of paediatric cancer. It draws on my experience as a father and touches on bigger themes that arose from my many conversations with Millie since the time her treatment ended.

Before we start exploring questions about cancer and many others relating to Millie's journey, I feel it's important to let you know what this book is, and is not, about. I want to be honest with you from the start so that you know exactly what you are in for.

I'll start with the use of the word *journey* to describe our experience as a family, collectively and as individuals, and where those individuals happen to be children, or in our case, my daughter. Improving cancer care for children is a key commitment of the NHS. Understanding and supporting patients' *journeys* – their experience of cancer and its treatment – marks an important shift, of late, in how the NHS seeks to deliver care for these patients. Several NHS trusts are adopting this more tailored patient-focused language when it comes to treating cancer, recognising there are many types of tumours and cancer, including brain cancer, that require different treatments. This can be true at every stage of the *journey*: from how medics identify symptoms, how a diagnosis is made, which hospital someone is referred to, the type of treatment they undertake, its length and, importantly, the patient's age. Even then, the journey might include what happens after treatment, which in paediatric cancer may span a lifetime for those lucky enough to survive this disease. I have adopted a *journey* metaphor here because I found it helpful, and it provides a framework for understanding how you cope with this particular affliction – an area I will explore in more detail.

While this book covers several aspects of my daughter's brain cancer, it is not specifically about this disease, and it's not even about paediatric cancer. It is about the many issues and practical challenges that parents, and survivors of childhood brain tumours (benign and malignant), face depending on the position of the tumour, its related treatment and cure, how the body copes with therapy and the level of support available in the recovery phase. Over the course of this book, I will, naturally, cover several areas often associated with cancer in children and brain tumours in particular. But I am neither a doctor, nor a paediatric oncologist, nor a molecular biologist. Rather, I explain what I know "medically" of this affliction as an informed layperson. My insights relate only to my experience of this illness, as a parent and a husband, and how it has affected my daughter, me and the lives of my wife and my other two children. I will touch on some of the basic facts about cancer, and how cancer is different in children, and why brain cancer specifically, and brain tumours generally, differ from other cancers. But I always write as an attentive non-specialist observer – not a professional – and only where it helps the broader understanding of the themes developed. No more, no less.

While this book is not a scientific nor a medical book, I will make reference to common scientific studies relating to paediatric brain cancer where they help explain the challenges and questions of a cancer diagnosis and its treatment. I provide reference literature for further exploration. I have taken care to validate my own grasp of the more complicated material with people far more knowledgeable than me, but any errors of judgment arising as a result of the conclusions I draw are entirely my own. I use a limited number of technical terms relating to cancer and its cure since it is difficult to avoid medical jargon entirely. So, you will encounter words like "protocol", "sequelae", "acute", "adjuvant chemotherapy", "glomerular" and so on. These terms are explained as I write, and I summarise them in a glossary of terms at the end.

While this book is not Millie's story, I have used the timeline of her treatment to blend and group into cohesive themes the essence of the conversations we had or the thinking they triggered as I considered choices, decisions and challenges during and after treatment. They were useful to me, as I contemplated how best to help Millie through some of the impasses of a cancer diagnosis, so I hope they will be useful to others.

Even though the book is divided into four sections, one for each season, this book is not strictly chronological in its approach. Why I chose seasons will soon become apparent.

Spring which sets the scene, will cover the first few days following the discovery of Millie's brain tumour and first brain operation. It seemed necessary to recount, in some detail, the first few days of her illness and the events which led up to it. It will mostly be my own voice you hear since Millie was then very young and most of her enquiries now relate to the nature of her disease, and the chronic health care needs she requires, rather than her time in hospital. Since she doesn't really remember that particular period in any great detail, she relies on what she has heard us describe.

Summer follows spring, naturally. Prepping Millie for chemotherapy follows her first operation. Here I look at how parents must adjust when cancer strikes a young child, the difference between our past, free of disease, and our future, filled with the practical, bodily implications of treatment. This section covers how the medical profession often tackles paediatric brain cancer and what chemotherapy for young children really means.

Autumn will see Millie undertake four gruelling cycles of chemotherapy and a second brain operation. Cancer treatment is never delivered in isolation. It is a hostile takeover of the body and affects the whole family, the siblings in particular. This section will cover many of the adverse side effects caused by brain cancer as well as those brought about by treatment and, more specifically, chemotherapy. Throughout this period, one of the main anxieties as a parent is whether treatment will ultimately be successful, and what it means if it isn't. The last chapter of part three looks at this in more detail.

Treating cancer is corrosive and produces long-lasting consequences for the body. **Winter** looks at how these are likely to affect Millie's health and quality of life over the course of her existence. How Millie views such limitations plays a crucial role in how she copes with the material after-effects of treatment and damage to the brain from the tumour itself. It takes time and the right support for both body and mind to recover from cancer and its treatment, especially from brain cancer which inevitably injures one of the body's most delicate organs. It changes life irrevocably for all involved. And the quality of Millie's long-term well-being will have been reduced as a result. The question is, how steeply?

But let me be very clear about the nature of this book. It is not an autobiographical sob story mostly concerned with my ostensible triumph over my, or Millie's, personal trauma. There is nothing triumphant or brave about coping with childhood cancer or supporting your daughter the best way you can to deal with this disease. Brave is when you have a choice, and I didn't choose for Millie to have cancer. Neither did she. I hope you will find no self-pity over the next few chapters. Of course, brain cancer is sad, especially when it happens to a seven-year-old. Of course, the treatment is significant and painful and difficult. Of course, we faced challenging choices and had to witness our daughter and her health deteriorate beyond recognition. But this book is not about that – it is about Millie, her treatment, the limitations it has imposed and what we found helpful in addressing and managing these during treatment and recovery. I hope that these reflections will help others facing similar situations and enduring similar hardships.

Accordingly, I was keen from the outset to ensure my narrative and observations were as honest and factual as possible. I knew at the onset that remaining objective would be difficult. Not through lack of trying but because I lived this tale. The anxiety I felt throughout the period of treatment and beyond may well have coloured some of my reflections during that time. They come from personal experience. I am not an outsider, and I am not emotionally detached from this particular narrative. This is a risk I have tried to mitigate in two ways.

Firstly, I want to be honest about my limited viewpoint. I have tried to be transparent about this predicament which arose from the traumatic events that I have lived through.

Experiencing and remembering can often be very different. When I remember the events of 2013, and those since the end of treatment to now, I am telling myself a constructed narrative of my life and that of my family. The two will have mixed in my mind. No doubt a story is often most important to us in how it ends since that affects how we remember it and appreciate its lessons. And this can be slightly different every time I recall how I think I might have felt and thought then, and how I *actually* felt and thought. This means the passage of time, and my memory's inherent limitations has already altered my recall relating to the period of Millie's treatment.

This is not so much a limitation for the parts of this book where I reflect on my conversations with Millie and write about their possible meanings and implications. I have been careful to capture the main elements of it shortly after they occurred. It is a problem when recalling the detail and the emotive impact of her complex cancer treatment which lasted over seven months and ended more than seven years ago. I certainly think I remember that time, but I probably can't remember it as I experienced it then.

This is a shortcoming I have tried to address using a diary I wrote at the time. When Millie was first diagnosed in April 2013, I started writing an account of what was happening. A few days after her first MRI scan, I began with an entry and would carry on writing notes until November 2013, when her treatment ended. These notes turned into a diary, often kept daily. What started out as a means to cope became more structured quite quickly. My main ambition was to record and preserve our story and its detail, so easily forgotten, so that Millie could read it later, to fully grasp its enormity. The diary, now completed, has a hundred entries – over seventy thousand words or so – covering the period from Friday, 5 April 2013, through to Saturday, 2 November 2013[3]. I record the details as I was experiencing the period of diagnosis and treatment, a factual record of the day-to-day as it unfolded. There was no retrospection; my writing was raw, unedited, the material of my memory.

Providing better insights on how my perspective between what I felt then and what I feel now has often changed was important to me because of the possible audience for this book. I imagine my readers will include survivors of childhood brain tumours, their parents and their clinicians, some of whom I know well. Survivors are not just data points on a graph; they are not just a collection of medical records. These are people we can have conversations with, people who love and are loved, people with joys and sorrows, and I wanted to be mindful of their expectations. Moreover, one such survivor may well be my own daughter should she choose to read it, now or in the future. I owe it to an older, adult Millie who might read the book and, I hope, be assured that I have represented her justly, honestly and fairly. So, I feel a deep moral responsibility to ensure my book remains factual and my reasoning sound as I recall Millie's cancer story and assess the impact of its cure.

Naturally, there is more than one way of describing the world of paediatric cancer. There is more than one way to attribute value and importance to some of the more salient issues developed here. I hope I have managed to remain balanced in my approach and I have highlighted moments where I felt my own bias as a parent threatened to distort the truth, or my poor grasp of complex clinical knowledge was getting in the way of a fair interpretation.

In the end, I will leave it to you, dear reader, to draw your own conclusion about whether I have succeeded or not. I certainly hope I have. For now, let's go back to the time when all this began.

INTRODUCTION

'What caused the bad cell in my head to grow, Daddy? And why did it make me blind?'

*

I don't remember precisely when my daughter Millie started asking me these questions. Like most beginnings, it was more of an emergent process that blossomed tentatively in November 2013 after the most acute phase of her brain cancer treatment. She was seven.

Up until then, Millie had been a very typical girl. She was born in a hurry in 2006 without too much fuss. Her older sister, Ellie, had accepted this new arrival with good grace, and it wasn't long before Luca – the third and final member of our procreative triumvirate – made his way into the world. Millie had enjoyed an ordinary upbringing without health niggles until a year before her diagnosis. We were a regular family with no more challenges than other young families in our position.

All that would change at 7:12am on 5 April 2013, when Millie woke up with, as she put it then, "fuzziness" in her eyes. I established quickly that she had, overnight, lost vision completely in her right eye and almost entirely in her left. After a morning of MRI scans, a brain cancer diagnosis soon followed. Over a period of seven months, she underwent three brain operations, four months of chemotherapy as a paediatric oncology ward's inpatient at Great Ormond Street Hospital and thirty sessions, over the last two months of treatment in October and November, of proton beam radiotherapy in Oklahoma City, USA.

Ever since our return from America in November 2013, we made a family habit of taking regular walks, often hiking along the many pinetum's trails at Bedgebury National Forest, a vast expanse of conifers of various shapes and sizes within the High Weald Area of Outstanding Natural Beauty, in South East England, not far from our home. The locals refer to it, proudly, as one of the "Seven Wonders of the Weald". Initially, these hour-long hikes were meant to rebuild Millie's lost strength and stamina after her three brain operations, four months of chemotherapy and two months of daily radiation to the head. They happened over a brief and brutal period of therapy which had begun the day Millie lost her vision. The reality of brain cancer and its cure changed our lives irrevocably but, even seven years later, how, and to what degree, remains unclear.

For a long time – both during and after treatment ended – Millie closed herself off from the world. A once talkative girl, full of fun and energy, she started turning inwards rather than outwards; the chatter stopped; the volume dimmed; her outlook altered.

This may have been a form of self-protection from a situation she did not understand but sensed was not normal for her age. It may have been the treatment's aggressive nature, sending her into a state of shock, which sapped every ounce of her energy. With the little she had left she may have directed it towards recovery rather than expressing her thoughts and feelings. Or perhaps it was because she was so young and cancer and its cure changed her physically, physiologically, and cognitively. Over seven months of intense therapy, it was possible she had become a stranger to herself. Her identity changed, and it would take some time for her to develop a way to cope and adapt to her new self.

Others around her probably started to treat her differently and so may have reinforced her perception that she needed to change how she saw herself. We, as parents, her siblings, the school and her peers, were also confronted by a "new" child, to whom we needed to react differently. Millie had cancer of the brain, the organ that defines us most as human beings, that contains our memories, our skills, our experiences, our emotions and our sense of self. And so, as Millie's behaviour changed, so did ours. Our family's desire to adapt to a new Millie may, in turn, have increased her propensity to see herself differently.

May, could, possibly, probably. Although we weren't dealing with an exact science, one thing was certain: Millie disconnected with the outside. She seemed lonely, helpless, and emotionally isolated.

Talking was difficult then and walking wasn't easy. Cancer and its treatment had taken their toll. Millie was generally weak, still recovering and on daily medications which affected her metabolic rate and energy levels. She needed motivation to put one foot in front of the other.

To distract Millie from the physical effort, I would often point out the pattern of leaves on a tree, the fluttering ribbons of petals, the shape a cluster of bluebells might make by the side of the path. Little by little, and with a few gently probing questions about her illness and the process of recovery, we stepped forward.

Over a few months of this new weekly schedule, going to Bedgebury became synonymous with talking about her cancer, the cure and its limitations. As Millie began to enjoy our routine, she needed less cajoling to walk and to talk. She began to eagerly anticipate these trips, even coming up with questions and topics of conversations before our weekly outings. The peaceful paths that carelessly wound their way amongst the soft shadows of trunks became, quite unexpectedly, a safe place where she could gain greater clarity about what had happened to her, rediscovering who she was, or even, who she had become.

Over the next few years after treatment, Millie and I visited the pinetum frequently where we talked about her illness, about suffering, about her cure and the limitations that disease and treatment would impose upon her. We talked about living and dying, about what made her sad and what made her happy, about family and friendships. We talked about life before cancer, about the present, about the future and about how to cope with the challenges of cancer and the aftermath of its treatment.

Along the forest trails, criss-crossing each other in increasingly familiar patterns, we covered a huge amount of ground on themes ranging from the significant to the trivial. Nothing was forbidden and all judgement was suspended. For that one hour, it was as if we weren't father and daughter but fellow travellers helping each other to find a way along the tortuous path to full recovery. It was a way home, with each walk inching us a little further, a little bit closer to being us again.

I learned so much from Millie as we meandered beneath the rows of chestnuts, birches, oaks and pines. I learned about my daughter's worries, concerns and anxieties. But she also offered her perspective on the limitations that cancer, and its treatment, would impose on her life. I discovered much about the consolations I was finding as I accepted that while life can never be perfect, we can strive to make it as comfortable, peaceful and worthwhile as possible.

We were able to recognise that sharing, especially the hard stuff, turned adversity from a burden into part of the necessary learning to become a better version of ourselves. For the first time since her diagnosis, we were able to look forward.

Much of the focus during treatment was on keeping Millie alive and minimising the risk of cancerous cells returning. Under the thin and delicate canopy of the Bedgebury woods, Millie could describe her desire for a future beyond just being safe and living longer. There, she could express hope for a chance to figure out her story and give her life meaning.

I wasn't quite prepared for these conversations to teach me quite so much about myself, such as the anxieties that had slowly penetrated every single corner of my mind. Millie's cancer had quite predictably taken its toll on me and the rest of my family. Among the trees, Millie's insights into her condition provided me with a new perspective, a deeper comprehension and even a reassurance that, gradually, she was developing her own coping strategies.

As a father, I felt a great responsibility to respond appropriately to Millie's questions and "reason-checking" queries. I began to look forward to our walks, that hour when the universe stood still and offered us a momentary sanctuary from our daily toils. For the first time during the most difficult, heart-wrenching period of my own existence, I felt liberated.

For a long time during treatment, we seemed to be walking on the very edge of life itself, on the border between death and a future worth living. A year later, I was walking with Millie for the sheer love of the moment, the wish to prolong it and the desire to provide her with the right answers. Since her diagnosis, I had been clear that Millie deserved honesty. Of course, I considered her age and her uncertainties about aspects of her condition in how I qualified my answers. It was equally important to balance these concerns with my obligation to be candid and reveal as much of the truth as I felt she could understand.

As you might expect, over the course of the five or six years we have walked and talked, Millie has matured. With each passing revolution of the earth around the sun, as nature painted and repainted the landscape with the emerald greens of conifers, the fiery hues of autumn scarlet and the quivering yellows of daffodil clusters, Millie became more sophisticated in her thinking and her questioning.

As we revisited questions from previous walks, we shaped and honed and defined our fears, our anxieties and our hopes. This thinking and rethinking allowed us to regain some control over our direction as we patiently examined the fragile content of our minds. We gained clarity and calm.

Our discussions circled around her illness, her recovery, how she felt about herself and how she was learning to cope with the limitations that the cure had left her with. We revisited areas already explored and, with each excursion, noticed more details of the nature around us, the little special imperfections: the distinctive curvature of a larch, the dark, diamond-shaped cracks on the bark of a silver birch by the lake's edge. And so it was with our chats. Similar questions yielded different answers, with new dimensions and an accumulating complexity as time passed. As the tree trunks around us grew, one layer at a time, so did our insight.

This book is my attempt to distil the essence of those conversations. They helped me make sense of a senseless situation, so I hope they might help others in similar circumstances.

Millie's cancer was my first real encounter with this illness and to say I wasn't prepared is an astronomical understatement. Nothing can prepare you for it. We were living in the moment while Millie was undergoing treatment, not knowing from one day to the next if she was going to pull through.

What I didn't appreciate then was the degree of permanent damage that the illness and its treatment would cause. Millie's cure was successful, but like the elimination of any cancer, it came at a significant cost. At some point, I realised that the end of childhood brain cancer treatment, and more generally treatment for brain tumours, wasn't an end at all. It marked instead the beginning of an arduous trek across an unpredictable, mostly unmapped forest, shrouded in darkness and doubt, with ambiguous forks pointing to untrodden paths.

Will cancer come back? To what degree will the latent effects of treatment, especially given the position of my daughter's tumour, affect her? Over how many years? How will this material event limit my daughter's life, now and in the future? How will time play out for her, with the collective complexities of her condition and the challenges she faces? Will she be afforded safe passage, or must I watch in anguish as the morbidities of long-term side effects take her before she reaches the evening of her life?

Walking while talking clarified these and many other questions. And it provided some relief for the unappeasable heartache that erupted when the diagnosis was confirmed. For a long time, my pain was the only thing I had left of a life before Millie's malignant brain tumour. As we walked, her soft voice swayed to the rhythm of the wind like a soothing balm for my sorrows, a future tense, a road ahead. I owe her that much and so much more.

Millie played a large part in how I managed to keep it together. At the chancy intersections of life, death and meaning, I don't know that I would have coped without the help of my daughter, my wife Vanessa and Ellie and Luca. I hope I have been a good father and husband to them in return; it hasn't always been easy, but I have tried my best. I hope I was able to answer the questions Millie has sent in my direction over the last six or seven years in the most appropriate way. And, finally, I hope the conversation will continue for many, many more years as I relish the delectable challenge of her frequent examinations.

*

'Those are great questions, Millie,' I say, contemplating which trail to take today, which line of reasoning to adopt. 'Let me tell you first about cells, how they grow and how they are able to replace old dead cells in your body.'

PART ONE
SPRING

THEMES

Coping with traumatic events. Dealing with uncertainty. Paediatric brain cancers: what are they exactly? Why do they happen? The nature of choice when children are involved. Talking to children about cancer.

It was one of those March days when the sun shines hot and the wind blows cold: when it is summer in the light, and winter in the shade.

GREAT EXPECTATIONS
CHARLES DICKENS

SUBTLE SIGNS OF CANCER

Shortly after the start of spring 2013, on Tuesday, 9 April, at 9:49am and less than a fortnight after Millie turned seven, Vanessa and I were given the news that she had brain cancer.

It was our first conversation with her paediatric oncologist, Dr H, and my first conversation, ever, with an oncologist. And it was our first meeting with this particular consultant over four very difficult days at Great Ormond Street Hospital (GOSH) in London. It took place in one of the quiet rooms on Koala Ward.

There is nothing unusual about the appearance of this ward, located on level six, or its other twenty-four individual rooms. Its plain walls are brightened by peaceful drawn-out scenes – cartoon style – of smiling fauna and colourful flora, and each ward is named after an animal to make it child-friendly. On this floor, the theme is koalas and their "babies", and it houses the hospital's inpatient neurosurgical department. Here, the children mostly require surgery to their faces, heads, brains or spines for conditions such as craniofacial abnormalities or disfigurements, epilepsy and, more pertinently for us, brain tumours.

Dr H was going to lead the multidisciplinary team of specialists my daughter would require over the coming months. After introducing himself briefly, he gave us what is sometimes referred to as the "day one talk" when cancer is concerned. Even though this wasn't day one for us, I guess it was the first time the diagnosis was confirmed.

'Following a review of her tumour marker results from recent blood samples,' he started, tentatively, 'Millie's tumour is not an astrocytoma or a craniopharyngioma as initially thought.' Astrocytomas and craniopharyngiomas are two different types of brain tumour. More on those later. 'We think it's a secreting germ cell tumour,' he continued. 'It's rare. Only ten children a year are diagnosed with it in the UK. And it's malignant.'

I didn't know what a secreting germ cell tumour was, but I knew Millie had cancer. I repeated the word senselessly in my head, numb with the pain of the previous four days in this hospital, trying to figure out a plan. The four worst days of what will turn out to be the worst period of our lives, so far. I should have been devastated by this new revelation but wasn't. The truth is, I was relatively unmoved since I had been so emphatically knocked out by the tragic events of the preceding seventy-two hours or so. I was still somewhat dazed. I was on the metaphorical floor being slow-counted and unable to get up. Who knew that even pain seems to adhere to the law of diminishing marginal return? At a certain point, adding bad news on top of bad news, punch after punch in quick succession, causes relatively smaller increases of hurt. I managed to get up that day. Eventually. But I still haven't recovered from this particular beating.

Millie had *cancer*. She was seven and she had cancer. Of the rarest kind. How could this happen? How could her tumour have grown without us noticing? Over years, probably. Unstoppable in its advance. Unrelenting in its enlargement. Unrepentant of the damage it had already caused. Undiscerning in how it selected this particular victim. Like many before us, we had been unable to read the signs until the inevitable happened: a precipitous admission to GOSH four days earlier, after seven years of tranquil, cancer-free living.

*

In Millie's case, the first signs happened broadly at the same time, approximately twelve months before diagnosis.

Early in 2012, she started to develop an excessive thirst and went from, mostly, dry nights to requiring two changes of nappies. She was drinking more and urinating more frequently. Her drinking was less like sipping and more like guzzling, even attaching herself to a small plastic bottle of water and literally sucking it dry.

This was clearly concerning, so we booked an appointment with her paediatrician, Dr D, who mentioned a condition, diabetes insipidus: a rare disease where you pee a lot and often feel thirsty as a result of chemical deficiencies, specifically, the lack of an antidiuretic hormone produced by the hypothalamus and released in the body via the pituitary gland. However, Dr D did not feel this was likely as "children with this condition are often very unwell". But the matter was considered serious enough that we were referred to a paediatric endocrinologist, a specialist who treats diseases affecting glands and the natural processes they control in the body by producing hormones. He had an office in Harley Street and was, reputedly, one of the top private specialists who had come highly recommended and had been associated with GOSH before retiring from active hospital duty.

He was keen to dismiss the more obvious possible conditions such as diabetes (of the more common kind), and a blood test confirmed Millie did not have this. Diabetes insipidus[4] was discussed, but he didn't feel Millie necessarily suffered from this either. He asked us strange questions like, "does she drink water out of plant pots or fishbowls or flushing cisterns?" since some children with this affliction apparently do. She looked too well, too normal, too healthy, he said, for thirst to strongly correlate with a serious condition. I was later told, by someone far more knowledgeable, that if their thirst is not compromised, such as by having access to drinking water, they do not become ill nor do they look ill. This is, apparently, a common misconception amongst general practitioners who only see these children at the very late stage of this condition. In fact, excessive thirst is among the possible symptoms to watch out for in the diagnosis of childhood brain tumours. Maybe the Harley Street "expert" was incompetent, or half asleep, or generally distracted and made complacent by years spent investigating what would mostly turn out to be inconsequential ailments. Or maybe he was just disinterested. People sometimes make mistakes. We'll never know.

But he was not overly concerned and since he felt the matter was mostly behavioural, he suggested a urine concentration test that we could conduct at home. The slightly more involved water depravation test, which required an overnight stay in hospital, wasn't needed at this stage. And there was certainly no mention of brain tumours or scans. We left in an optimistic mood, taking his judgment at face value, as you should with experts.

The urine concentration test was hard for Millie. We had to stop her drinking from the time she went to bed, till the morning. Only then could a clean-catch urine sample be taken for analysis. The first test was inconclusive since Millie had probably had a drink in the night, which would have invalidated the results. At a second visit to the endocrinologist, a further urine concentration test was prescribed. This time, I stayed with Millie throughout the night to prevent her from ingesting any kind of liquid. She spent most of the night semi-awake, asking me, frequently, for a drink of water. Eventually, 6am arrived, and we could gather a sample.

The results, this time, were also inconclusive; Millie's thirst remained insatiable and her nightly urine output high. It was now affecting her so that she couldn't go on school trips without needing to stop for frequent loo breaks. On holidays abroad, after finishing the supply of bottles on her bedside in the evening, she would roam the hotel room, looking to quench her raging thirst. Even during breaks nearer home, she became anxious about having access to water.

Millie, at the same time, began to lose concentration at school. There were good days when she could engage in a lesson and others when she just wanted to be left to rest quietly in a corner. Her energy levels fluctuated so regularly that her teacher described it to us as teaching "two different Millies".

And yet, there didn't seem to be anything drastically wrong with her. Vanessa and I never felt the same urgency we would feel when Millie was eventually diagnosed with brain cancer. How could we be so blind? Why didn't we spot this earlier? How could this escape the natural filter of our parental instinct or even the application of good judgement? We kept reassuring ourselves she was navigating the day-to-day perfectly well, going to school, eating (and drinking!) and playing with her brother and sister. We knew something was wrong; we just didn't know what. And since no one had been able to tell us, we simply hoped for an easy resolution.

Since there even remained a faint possibility that this was a behavioural issue, we tried the parental strategy of "reward for good behaviour". Millie was keen to get a 3DS, a handheld gaming console popular at the time, so we struck a deal: if she could limit her drinking and stay dry for three successive nights, we would buy it for her. A strategy that had worked with her own father long, long ago, though with a far less glamorous toy. Incidentally, yours truly did manage three dry nights in a row, received the much coveted, promised toy – a sit-on orange digger – and happily resumed bed-wetting for another year or so thereafter, or so the family myth goes...

But Millie never managed it, and the reason why would soon be agonisingly obvious. At the time, however, we interpreted it differently. You see, bed-wetting in childhood has an hereditary element to it. As many as seventy-five per cent of reported cases have a parent or sibling that wet the bed in childhood beyond an age that might be considered the norm. This, of course, reinforced our belief – or what we wanted to believe – that it was nothing serious. Nonetheless, we booked a third appointment with the endocrinologist to determine what next steps we might need to get to the bottom of it all.

The likely procedure following an ambiguous result in her urine sample was going to be a water deprivation test. We knew this would require a day or two of hospitalisation so that Millie could be deprived of water for a day and a night while regular blood tests were taken. Since this risked dehydration, she needed to be closely monitored in the right environment.

For Easter that year, we would visit my parents in the north of Italy so booked an appointment with Dr D, on the day after our return, 5 April 2013. It was a precaution before the start of term, though against what we weren't sure.

Millie had been subdued throughout our brief trip to *Nonno* and *Nonna*'s house, and we all flew back on Thursday, 4 April. As our plane formed a soft arc across European skies, the path of our own lives was about to take an abrupt dive into a harsh terrain. And one that we would never leave.

*

Cancer survivors, and parents of childhood cancer survivors, often talk about omens overlooked or the missing of subtle messages that the disease and its progression were sending in the time before diagnosis. Like faint distress signals emitted by the body but discounted as vague, non-threatening symptoms by both parents and health professionals. In fact, the early diagnosis of paediatric brain tumours is extremely rare in primary care: the child's GP or paediatrician. Brain tumours often present with such varied, non-specific warnings, and so doctors tend to make other, more likely diagnoses. It actually forms part of their training. They're often taught 'when you hear hoofbeats, think horses not zebras,' meaning a doctor should first think about what is a more common – and potentially more likely – diagnosis.

A Bristol University study from 2018[5] analysed how different symptoms predict differences in the time primary carers take to diagnose brain tumours. With data from some eighteen thousand patients, across over a thousand practices in some twenty cancer networks in the UK, its authors concluded that rapidly diagnosing brain tumours is challenging because its symptoms are often mild and non-specific. Reassuringly for us parents, the same study also suggests that delays in diagnosis may not have detrimental effects on the outcome of treatment, nor whether it impacts on the efficacy and morbidity of therapies. Even so, diagnosing this particular illness at a late stage certainly causes additional anxiety for parents when a brain tumour is finally confirmed.

Looking back, it is quite clear that diabetes insipidus was an important and sinister clue that might have justified an earlier scan to the midbrain. The endocrinologist should have thought Zebras. The thirst, the lack of energy, the excess elimination of fluid were direct causes of the damage by the tumour to the hypothalamus and pituitary gland as it gathered volume within the skull's narrow confines. About a month before our trip to Italy, Millie did in fact suffer from a painful headache that ebbed and flowed before it disappeared.

As she recalls this time, Millie does not remember that she was afraid or alarmed by her excessive thirst. Instead, she recalls little of that year before diagnosis, perhaps comforted by her parents' attitude. Whilst Vanessa and I were concerned about her health, we did not want to upset her and so minimised its possible causes. Not that brain cancer was on that list.

Naturally, we have often wondered whether we were forceful enough in our requests for further investigations or if we had best represented Millie's health interests. Should we, collectively – us as parents, her paediatrician and the endocrinologist – have grasped much earlier the need for a more thorough examination, such as a brain scan. Would discovering her tumour earlier have made any difference to the overall outcome of her treatment?

These are questions Millie asks frequently, and my answers can only be speculative, abstract and unsatisfactory. Perhaps it makes no sense to try and answer them at all. Aside from one main element which I will cover shortly, the application of the treatment and its outcome – including all its side effects – would have most likely been the same.

These questions and thoughts, that have often been too deep for tears, have been reverberating ever since in the echo chamber of my life's regrets. And I have examined them without reaching a resolution, on many late nights in the GOSH paediatric oncology ward, on a small bed, next to Millie's where she lay, being injected with poison to melt the cancer growing within her.

Despite my anguish, I sense, or at least hope, it would be wrong to feel guilt. We are, after all, seldom the author of our lives, and most of us fall foul of the creeping determinism that informs our tendencies to perceive such events as more predictable than they actually are before they occur. Hindsight bias, which is nothing new. This powerful force is often applied in medical diagnosis. We often recall information selectively. We cherry-pick only those elements that help us weave a narrative we know makes sense against the outcomes we know to be true. The story was easy to tell, with Millie and her symptoms; we believed that the outcome was foreseeable, and we should have known, all along, that it was cancer.

Of course, this psychological bias is particularly prevalent amongst parents of childhood brain tumour survivors because of the very nature of the affliction. I have met many of these parents whose narratives, like mine, only make sense in retrospect.

There is a reason for this. Many early neurological symptoms that might suggest a brain tumour have a low predictive value. They can often also point to more common and benign conditions. The other problem is the sheer number of possible signs attributable to such diagnoses. One study[6] that analysed primary health care records in the UK identified more than twenty relevant signs of brain tumour including back problems, emotional difficulties such as school phobia, sleep disturbance, "unhappiness" and headaches.

This spectrum of possible warnings makes early brain tumour diagnosis very problematic for GPs and even specialists who still struggle to recognise early warning signs. As laypeople, what chance did we have then, really? Such diagnostic challenges are compounded in children who adapt much better than adults to changes in their physical and mental conditions. They are better at hiding symptoms from doctors and parents and less able to articulate what they might be experiencing. This is even more difficult when a child experiences imperceptible neurological and physiological changes which could mean a hundred other more probable ailments rather than clearly identifiable symptoms. Or when a correct diagnosis requires a medic to identify the one amongst the thirty-three thousand children in the UK per year who shares with so many others the common expression of a much more pedestrian illness.

The reality, regrettably, is that brain tumours in children are, generally, not diagnosed until the symptoms start causing real physiological damage. Such symptoms vary from severe, continuous headaches, to seizures, drowsiness, vomiting, hearing loss, hearing voices, weaknesses in arms or legs. The list goes on. This results mostly from increased pressure inside the skull where the extent of the tumour's damage depends on its position and proximity to its neighbouring structures.

People, and children, tend to experience small, progressive, cumulative changes rather than symptoms. Changes that are often noticed by others, rather than those close to the sufferer. Except for the thirst, Millie's changes seemed subtle and disconnected from each other. Like the frog in the fable, we were slowly being boiled alive, unaware of the ultimate danger. Millie's golf-ball-sized lump was discovered when the tumour affected her vision and overnight, she went blind.

THE DAY WHEN
EVERYTHING CHANGED

'Bad news I'm afraid – it's a brain tumour.'

This brief statement was spoken soberly by Millie's paediatrician, Dr D, shortly after 12:30pm on Friday, 5 April, approximately four days before our first encounter with her oncologist.

He spoke deliberately, steadily. At first, I didn't hear the sound of the words but saw them float slowly across the room and against the wet, discoloured droplets weeping down the windowpane behind his desk. It was raining outside.

This handful of words still resonates in the saddest recesses of my soul, in a place only I can hear it.

*

The day when everything changed had started badly. Millie had been somewhat lethargic during our trip, the day before, back home from my parent's house in Italy. She woke up and, with tentative apprehension, told me her eyes were a bit "fuzzy". She seemed a little confused. I was not overly concerned since having my three children has induced resistance to thinking the worst about such statements.

So, we sat down on the sofa in our kitchen and started a few "how many fingers" tests. It didn't take long before I realised that she could no longer see from her right eye – "I can just see brown, Daddy" – and could only make out a few fingers from her left eye. The following morning, I discovered that she had lost vision completely in her right eye and almost entirely in her left.

After her peaceful night, that morning, the sun did not rise for Millie. For some reason, a darkness set in.

Strangely, the traumatic nature of this event didn't seem to bother Millie hugely. She appeared serene, responding to my enquiries matter-of-factly. She was unaware of the shadows beginning to rise in the very core of my being. I tried not to panic, to avoid alarming Millie. I looked back at Vanessa, then at Millie. We were suspended in disbelief. I repeated a few fingers tests as if wishing, somehow, that her inaccuracies were lapses of concentration. No such luck.

We all have, generally, good recollection of where we were, or what we were doing, when we experienced emotionally significant events. Good ones such as birthdays, getting up really early in the morning for a journey on holiday, playing on a rope swing in the woods or a first kiss with a magical girl under the warm glow of sundown over the peaceful, uninterested landscape of Knole Park in the summer of 1989. But bad ones too tend to leave a permanent deposit on the memory bank, like being in this kitchen, sitting next to Millie, sensing that the world as we knew it was never going to be the same again.

I've heard adrenaline helps to consolidate, like a fixing agent, significant events in our long-term memory. A different kind of theory of relativity operates: our perception of time slows down while everything inside us speeds up; the heart beats faster; the blood flow increases. All to prepare our body and mind to cope with extraordinary circumstances. Nature's way of making sure I felt like I lived this moment for longer than it lasted – nature's way of cementing the pain, the anguish, the fear, the confusion. But also, her way of ensuring I understood the significance of the moment, the need for focus. For Millie's sake.

I was experiencing a toxic cocktail of feelings. And yet, amid the confusion, I was acutely aware my senses were beginning to sharpen, my body responding in its most primal form of fight or flight. A protective instinct for my offspring perhaps. Everything inside me was screaming a forewarning of what was to come.

Then, it was time to focus.

Given we had an appointment in London with Millie's paediatrician, Dr D, later that morning, Vanessa and I decided on balance that it was best to keep it rather than take her straight to the local hospital's A&E. We considered this but, under the circumstances, it didn't feel like the right thing to do. Dr D knew us; he knew Millie and her medical history; and he had good contacts with relevant specialists. If we needed to move quickly, we felt confident he would facilitate whatever action was required.

I remember Millie and I catching the 7:40am to Charing Cross while Vanessa stayed home with our other two children. Millie was quiet, subdued. I carry her everywhere because, by now, it is clear she can't see. I feel a shadow following me everywhere I go, one that has seldom left me. With time, I have simply grown better at ignoring its presence.

Dr D's consulting room is located at the top of Great Portland Street, near the tube station bearing the same name. He sees us relatively quickly but, initially, this consultation doesn't go as I had planned. We start by reviewing progress on the thirst. He suggests a brain scan might be worthwhile, at some point. This is the first time he has mentioned a brain scan since we reported Millie's excessive thirst about a year ago.

I then explain the morning's misadventures, which, at first, Dr D does not seem too worried about. 'A bit of blurry vision is possibly a bit of tiredness; she seems well otherwise. Let's keep in touch to review progress.' Did I say it right? Am I worrying for nothing? For an iota of a split second, I allow myself to feel some relief, thinking of getting up, shaking his hand and going back home with Millie. Thankfully, my instincts don't allow it. Looking back, the possibility that I might have done – with all the consequences that would have resulted from it – is something that every now and then worms its way into my mind, in the early hours, when these types of thoughts often catch us unaware.

When I repeat the obvious, 'what about the fact that she cannot see at all from one eye and barely from the other?', his expression changes.

'It's not good,' he says.

It takes him only one phone call to arrange an emergency MRI scan at the Portland Hospital, across the road. Millie and I leave his consulting room and cross Great Portland Street. At the hospital reception, a nurse hands us an information leaflet with some basic dos and don'ts about MRIs. Because the scan uses a large strong magnet to create radio waves and a computer to form an image of your body, these instructions relate mostly to removing any metallic objects and bank cards. Millie is comforted that MRI scans are painless, and the equipment doesn't seem to worry her too much. The machine itself looks like a large, white tube and some children (and adults for that matter – I had one not long ago) can find the experience somewhat claustrophobic.

Millie is offered headphones and a film to watch to cover the noise of the MRI. The thought doesn't really occur to us that she can't see much at this stage. After only three hours into this nightmare, our compass is still firmly set in a world untainted by cancer, so she chooses *Mary Poppins*, the original, somewhat instinctively and to the tune of 'A Spoonful of Sugar' (the irony does not escape me), the moveable bed on which she is lying, slowly drifts her headfirst into the circular tube and a very uncertain future.

While the scan itself is painless, a contrast or dye is often injected intravenously to improve the quality and detail of the images. Millie isn't so happy about that, though she doesn't know that it's the first of many such injections.

I convince her to have it by promising to buy her a game console, the one I had held out in the hope of improving the wet nights situation. She reluctantly agrees. The scan lasts approximately thirty minutes, and as Millie slides out again, the nurses tell me to return to Dr D's office to await the results. I realise that they have already spotted what he will later confirm to me. What their words do not reveal, their eyes cannot conceal. With a sense of overwhelming anguish which turns light into dark, we cross the road to Dr D who confirms the diagnosis.

He can't be specific about the type of tumour deep inside Millie's brain, but he understands we must act quickly. Firstly, he will start the process of admitting us at Great Ormond Street Hospital. He needs confirmation that GOSH have been made aware of our situation, so the plan is for Millie and me to deliver the CD with the scan to Mr J, its leading neurosurgeon, later that day. It's the first time I hear his name, unaware of the substantial contribution he will make that week towards giving Millie a life worth living.

Secondly, Dr D wants to address, or at least slow down, the cause of Millie's loss of sight. He believes that the tumour is compressing the optic nerves, possibly caused by an inflammatory reaction to a likely lesion of the tumour mass itself. Given that she has lost sight in both eyes, the lesion is probably occurring at, or in and around, the optic chiasm where some of the fibres from half of each retina cross over, broadly in the midbrain, and proceed to opposite ends of the visual cortex at the back of the head.

Dr D prescribes a strong steroid called dexamethasone to decrease the body's natural defence response and reduce symptoms such as swelling. This will be the first of many drugs Millie will take over the next few months, and thankfully, it can be taken orally.

Millie is still unaware of the seriousness of her condition. At some point, I know I will have to explain, somehow, the nature of her illness and its likely consequence that she may never recover her eyesight and may remain visually impaired. At the moment, I don't even know how to begin to contemplate this conversation. And, anyway, I don't know enough myself at this stage, so it can wait. I do let her know, however, that we may need to go to a hospital, a very good one for children. They will need to look at her scan and see what they must do to make her better. We may be spending a bit of time in hospital, but she is not to worry as Mummy and Daddy will be there with her all the time.

She listens, very calmly, and then tells me she's hungry. We won't hear back from GOSH for a couple of hours, so we cross the road to a Pizza Express.

I am conscious that I must update Vanessa on the diagnosis. So, on the way to our pizza, I make the most difficult phone call I have ever had to make. I need to let Vanessa know her little girl has a brain tumour, that it's clearly very serious and that we are trying to get to GOSH to understand what we need to do next. And that Millie, all of us, in fact, are facing a very uncertain future and the possibility that we may lose her altogether over the coming weeks or months. At this stage, that's all I really know.

I dial her number.

WHEN NOTHING IS SURE

Uncertainty is probably the most difficult element to navigate during the initial phases of investigation of a brain tumour diagnosis. It took four days of tests, scans, waiting, more tests, more scans, a nine-hour long brain operation and yet more scans and more waiting before we had final confirmation of exactly what we were facing and what we were likely to confront in the months ahead. It may not seem long, but the four days was agonising, turning minutes into hours, and hours into months.

Even though Millie had seemed relatively tranquil throughout the first day, I wonder how she must have been feeling. Was she sensing the storm rising within me? The fear? The doubt? The possible outcomes of her illness, including the possibility of dying? I can only hope she was not suffering as much as I was at that moment, that her age allowed some natural shelter against the cruel, unfavourable and ultimately random whims of chance.

*

We often talk about that day, during our frequent walks. I sense Millie doesn't remember it. She does recall her "fuzziness" and claims to recollect the moment her eyesight faded. But it seems clear she is calling to mind the grown-ups' description of the event as she has heard it from them. To start with, she was very young. What do I remember of my time as a seven-year-old? I never lost my eyesight, and more time has passed since then for me than it has for Millie, but I would struggle to remember anything specific.

Moreover, her memory of it seems too consistent between one recollection and another. There is something artificial in how she reminisces about 5 April 2013. She's not travelling back in time, nor remembering an actual event, but merely recalling the memory of the last time we spoke about it or the time before then. The same happens when I remember it. All of this remembering and talking about it may well have distorted and transformed not just our memory but our feelings about it then, and now, and every slice of time in-between.

There's a paradox here. The very memories we treasure, the happy ones, the ones we retrieve more often because they comfort us, are also the ones we're likely to have changed the most, by the very act of revisiting them, again and again. They lack fidelity to the real event. This may be a good thing. Millie was seven when the worst happened and much of her memory may be shaped by the narrative we have constructed around her since. By the things she has heard us say or has seen us do. We have had a very direct role to play not just in how she looks back at the event itself, but her perception of it. How she feels about it.

With a little effort, we have deliberately reinforced the positives of her diagnosis: her resilience, her resolve and how she handled treatment in the most amazing way. I have no doubt that over the past seven years, this has shaped her worldview, her character and perhaps how she might contemplate her future.

But I digress.

For now, let's just say that Millie probably does not remember in detail much about the day her life changed forever, nor is she likely to carry with her the anxiety she must have felt. What's clearer is that Vanessa and I can easily revive a detailed chronology of the day Millie went blind and her brain tumour diagnosis was confirmed. It was the day before she was admitted to GOSH and before her first nine-hour long craniotomy, a fancy word for brain surgery.

*

Vanessa is not normally quick to pick up the phone. She often claims this is due to a decline in hearing as a result of a hereditary condition, or malfunctioning technology, or that something's wrong with her phone, or a random combination of the above. This time it's different. She picks up after one ring. I update her as best I can on my conversation with Dr D and probably kill a little bit of her, just as a bit of me died when I heard the diagnosis. Pragmatic as always, she tells me she has organised for Ellie and Luca to stay with their grandmother and aunt. For now, all we can tell them is that Millie must spend a few days in hospital to help her eyes but that they should not worry.

With this arrangement in place, we can focus on Millie and whatever comes at us over the next hours and days.

The uncertainty doesn't extend just to not knowing what is likely to unfold. It also applies to the detail of the diagnosis and both its short and long-term implications.

As we gather our thoughts during that phone call, and later that evening, after Millie and I have returned from London and we await confirmation of admission to GOSH, it becomes clear that for regular parents like us, the initial currency of a brain tumour diagnosis is ignorance. An ignorance that is filled by deep anxiety about our daughter's well-being.

Whilst we know Millie has a brain tumour, we don't know what type, nor how many types there might be. We realise the sinister and serious nature of her diagnosis, but we don't know how serious or how sinister. We know tumours can be benign or malignant (cancerous), but which one does Millie have? We don't know what treatment might be required, over how long, where and how it might affect Millie. We don't even know if we will be admitted to GOSH – though we sincerely hope so – and whether it is the right place for her. We know this will have a material impact on Millie's life, at best, but we don't know its nature or the degree to which the quality of it will be changed. (We suspect it will be for the worse.) We don't know if Millie will ever regain her eyesight, which hasn't improved that day and with which she can only see through a tiny window from her right eye.

Perhaps more distressing, we don't know how long she will be with us but know this could take her life within a relatively short period. My daughter could soon die from something deep inside her skull, something obscure and inexplicable at this stage. A desperately horrifying possibility I haven't even begun to process.

Nightfall brings this awful day to an end, and it will be a while before we perceive the odd, dim ray of light breaking through the dense and fetid thickness of our future. Exhausted by the day, Millie has no difficulty in going to sleep. Scared and confused, she may have possessed questions she was too young to articulate and too little to resolve.

What's a brain tumour?
Why can't I see?
Why me?

A RARE MALIGNANT TUMOUR

The date on the letter from the Department of Haematology and Oncology at GOSH is 13 April 2013. It is written by Dr H, Millie's oncologist, and the first formal correspondence from GOSH since we were admitted on 6 April. Because of various conventions and protocols, it's not addressed to me but to my local GP in East Sussex. It is the first written confirmation of Millie's illness and summarises the events of the last week. After some initial background on Millie and her symptoms on admission, it goes on to say the following:

I explained to Millie's parents that the provisional diagnosis from the tumour markers was of a rare malignant (cancerous) tumour known as a secreting suprasellar intracranial germ cell tumour.

Rare. Tumour markers. Malignant. Secreting. Suprasellar. Germ cell.

I read and reread these words unable to grasp the enormity of their significance. Of the detail, the implication they have, for us, for Millie. What does this all mean?

A challenging aspect of a brain tumour diagnosis is our lack of knowledge as parents, laypeople, about the tangled maze of cancer and its multiform treatments. It's a complex world even for medical researchers and clinicians who spend their time navigating the convoluted language and biochemistry of oncological treatments and cures. Over time, I did become more familiar with some details, numbers and statistics of cancer and gained a basic understanding of its nature, forms and particular medical jargon, as well as the broader issues arising from brain tumours and the consequences for sufferers, their loved ones, their carers and the medical professionals who dedicate their professional careers to minimising its impact on people's lives.

*

So, what is paediatric cancer and childhood brain cancer in particular? Millie asks me this frequently as she seeks to make sense of her illness. It's possible that, rationalising cancer's biology will enable her to better come to terms with it all. Children often need some sense of agency or causality for events they don't understand but which directly affects their lives.

When children look for an explanation for improbable events in particular, they need an even more special explanation, some additional reason to suggest that the improbable event is not just due to bad luck, to chance. I sense it's why Millie's questions, on our walks, often start with a "why?": "why did this happen to me?", "why did my brain cancer make me lose my eyesight?", "why aren't brain tumours all treated in the same way?", "why did the bad cell grow into a lump?", "why was it there in the first place?". To provide clear answers, I have always made great efforts to remain factual. We have often talked about the words on Dr H's letter which provide scaffolding for thinking about childhood cancer generally and brain cancer more specifically.

So, let's do the same here and start with "rare".

All childhood cancers – let alone brain cancers[7] – are rare, far rarer than a single adult cancer type taken on its own. By some distance. So, all children with all types of cancer taken together are fewer than the number of adults for only one type of cancer. Any type.

A quarter of all childhood cancers are brain tumours. They are the second most common childhood malignancy in children, behind leukaemia[8], a type of blood cancer. They do beat leukaemia as being the most common type of solid tumour in children and unfortunately, the most common cause of death among all childhood cancers.

So how rare is rare? The latest official data available about cancer in the UK dates back to 2016-2018, courtesy of Cancer Research UK[9]. Broadly, 375,400 people in the UK, children and adults, are diagnosed with one type of cancer every year. This means that, every day of the year, 1,028 people in the UK will be given a cancer diagnosis (or at least they were in the years leading up to 2016-2018). On average, this represents a death sentence within ten years for one in every two of them.

That's everyone combined. Cancer, as a recent advert explains, does not discriminate, unless you are in a high-risk group like smokers.

Of those 375,400 yearly diagnoses, 1,838 are children

(that's 0.005%…). And out of that group, 460, give or take, are children with a malignant brain tumour diagnosis (0.001%…). Put another way, of those 1,028 people diagnosed every day with a type of cancer, five are children. And of those five children, one of them – just over actually, statistically speaking – will receive a brain cancer diagnosis. That's one child a year for every thirty-three thousand healthy children and adolescents in the UK. If your average football stadium capable of welcoming, say, some sixty thousand supporters, represented all people under nineteen in the UK in any given year, three hundred of them will have cancer. Two out of those three hundred would be children with a brain tumour diagnosis.

Millie was one of those two.

Not just bad luck but bad luck on an astronomical scale. There was no rhyme nor reason for her brain cancer, which is something Millie struggles to come to terms with. Her cells were not saturated with malevolent purpose or a corrupt desire to develop cancer. We, or she, didn't do anything in her lifetime to increase the propensity for one of her cells to start its pattern of uncontrolled and rapid growth. There is no freedom from fate or chance. Shit, as they say, happens.

In addition to their low incident rate, central nervous system (CNS) tumours are both extraordinarily diverse in terms of their make-up (their "tumour biology" since tumours and cancers within the brain can, for example, arise from very different cell types and require different types of chemotherapy) but also in terms of their location.

Malignancies can spread from the brain to the spine, traveling down the central nervous system that connects the brain to the rest of the body. For me, this was another potentially significant revelation which was spelled out in the letter:

There is a possibility that they [malignant tumours] can spread through the CSF [cerebrospinal fluid].

CSF is a clear, colourless body fluid found in the brain and spinal cord and, luckily for Millie, the tumour had not spread, since this would have reduced considerably her chances of survival and required a more comprehensive irradiation.

The differences in tumour location and tumour biology are reasons that defective cells require the application of different treatment protocols. But more particularly, they explain why brain cancer can produce so many different symptoms at diagnosis and in its so-called latent side effects, often material and life-long.

So, childhood brain cancer is rare but also complicated. Brain cancer, like any type of cancer, isn't just one disease but many.

Historically, CNS tumours have been grouped according to what they looked like when viewed under a microscope[10]. This may seem parochial these days. More recently, this classification has been tweaked to reflect progress made in understanding tumour biology. Scientists are now beginning to focus more on molecular parameters, as opposed to just relying on what a bunch of cells might look like when spread out on a microscope glass slide, their "histological" appearance. This is helpful for all sorts of reasons. Cancer cells are cells first and foremost, and anti-cancer drugs target weaknesses in different types of cancer cells. So, understanding cells at the molecular level helps scientists develop targeted treatments that can affect specific cancer cells in a certain way. More on that later.

According to this latest arrangement, fifteen different types of CNS tumours can be identified, and within each type, there are several subtypes. They are an obscure, murky and cryptic mob, with names to rival any good old-fashioned monster of classical mythology. Names like anaplastic oligodendroglioma, pilocytic astrocytoma or myxopapillary ependymoma. Where do they come from, these mysteriously named living tissues of bad stuff?

In a very general sense, CNS tumours broadly arise from things going wrong in the different types of cells in the brain. And generally, they bear the name of the cell type and area of the brain they originate from. For example, a lot of brain tumours start in the "glial" cells which are a specialised bunch that surround neurons – nerve cells – to provide support and insulation between them. They come in different types such as oligodendrocytes, astrocytes, ependymal cells etc. It follows that tumours arising from these types of cells are known as "gliomas" – from glial cells – and depending on the type of "glial" cell they originate from, they include tumours such as oligodendrogliomas (from oligodendrocytes), astrocytomas (from astrocytes) and ependymomas (from ependymal cells).

Other tumours come from embryonal cells that remain in the brain after birth (probably over-simplistic, but you get the gist). Medulloblastoma, which starts in or near the cerebellum, is a relatively well-known and deadly type. And there are several other, rarer ones, in this category. Some arise from meningeal tissue – the outer membranes that envelop the brain – and these are classified as meningiomas.

And then there are tumours that grow in the pituitary fossa – the little pocket of bone in the deep midbrain where the pituitary gland safely resides – the better known of these is a benign beast known as craniopharyngioma[11].

Before my personal encounter with childhood brain tumours, I had not heard of any of these, nor of their many qualifiers. Millie's, as the letter indicated, was a "suprasellar secreting germ cell tumour". Five words forever engraved in deep grooves on the more permanent recesses of my memory. Five nebulous words to describe a serious, life-threatening condition that would inexorably alter and define the whole of the rest of her life – probably not in a good way. Though she would have to survive it first.

I often look back with envy at my younger self – I know it's somewhat selfish – when those five words were unfamiliar to me, when the future I contemplated didn't have the word cancer in it, when I didn't have to think or cope with the irreversibility of time and the prospect of losing my daughter. When the problems I thought I had weren't problems at all.

This is what even Millie – and it breaks my heart that she does – now understands as a "suprasellar secreting germ cell tumour":

a) the tumour was located in the suprasellar region of the brain, the "sellar" being a little saddle-shaped, fluid-filled pocket of brain located more or less at the base of the skull, deep in the midbrain where the pituitary gland is located;

b) her tumour mass was sitting above it, "supra" being Latin for "above";

c) it was a germ cell tumour[12] in which the cells making up the lump originate from germ cells and left there, probably, at some point during embryonic development when a few straddling germ cells in and around the brain region didn't switch to doing what they were supposed to have done (some even develop into hair or teeth or other body organs – this wasn't the case for Millie's);

d) it was "secreting". This helped in confirming diagnosis and meant it was oozing two specific proteins into the bloodstream, known as tumour markers and often used to identify, and measure, how many of the cancerous cells are left in the body and known often by their shortened name of AFP and beta-hCG[13];

e) and it's complicated… in several ways. Firstly, by the need to get the tumour out in the first place – tricky when the location of the mass is the midbrain – and secondly, by cancer treatment that occurs over a long period of time and combines several types of therapies.

I was about to learn all of this the hard way.

Little is currently known about how brain cancers develop and why they arise in the first place. Indeed, there may not be a "why", and in my daughter's case, a meaningful causal explanation probably doesn't exist. The body, this phenomenally complex machine we often take for granted, sometimes does things a teeny tiny bit wrong. For Millie, a few rogue germ cells grown *in utero* were left where they didn't belong and slowly developed into a solid mass of malignant cellular clusters deep inside a specific region of her brain (for this type of tumour always in the same spot).

Other tumours can have contributing factors to their development, but whatever they are, they are still relatively poorly understood and need much more investigation and funding to undertake the necessary research to get to know them better. Perversely, and as an aside, one of the main known risks of brain tumour development – albeit very low – is exposure to radiation, one of the three main treatments used to eradicate these unwanted cellular masses, leaving children cured of brain tumours at higher risks of developing a secondary one post-treatment. Sometimes, life just isn't fair…

As I'll explain in more detail later, Millie would undergo a fairly typical – if somewhat brutal – treatment plan of surgery, chemotherapy and radiotherapy which is how most brain cancers are still treated. Surgical resection – physically removing all or part of the tumour by means of a brain operation called craniotomy – remains a dominant pillar of this three-tiered approach. If surgery is difficult, because of the tumour's presentation or location, for example, then treatment must rely more on chemotherapy or radiotherapy, or both. The application of each one of these three modes of treatment, and their combinations, depend on a number of variables. These include, but are not limited to: the type of tumour, its precise location, whether it is benign or malignant, the stage of the disease, the associated presenting symptoms and complications and the age of the child at diagnosis. Those elements are also significant because they tend to inform the possible long-term side effects of curing cancer which often come at a cost. They carry potentially devastating neurological, neurocognitive, hormonal and behavioural sequelae across the course of a child's entire development through to adulthood and beyond.

Childhood brain tumours, therefore, are rare and complex, requiring care of the most specialist kind, in beacons of paediatric excellence such as GOSH. To most parents, the science behind the cure and its application is unfathomably complicated and obscure. The organ affected, the brain, is one of the most sensitive and most vital of what makes us human. But behind each and every one of these stories of a tumour are children and their families who come face to face with the most pitiless, remorseless suffering in a bid to save lives and to preserve as much of themselves as the disease, or its cure, will allow.

In Millie's case, the "cure" started with a nine-hour long brain operation at GOSH, two days after she lost her eyesight, and to preserve as much of her vision as she had left.

CRANIOTOMY (NOUN):
SURGICAL REMOVAL OF PART OF
THE BONE FROM THE SKULL TO
EXPOSE THE BRAIN

'We could do nothing for the time being,' explains Mr J, GOSH's lead neurosurgeon, in the "quiet room", the small consulting cubicle near the entrance of the ward itself. 'Millie's tumour is not an immediate threat to her life. But craniotomies do not come without very big risks, including strokes, loss of life and severe life-long motor and neurological impairments. Her life does not depend on this operation.' He pauses. 'The urgency to operate is more to do with preserving her eyesight.'

Preserving... my mind lingers over that word. Millie is now as good as blind. Probably irreversibly. We had had confirmation of that earlier in the day when we were sent for an assessment, by GOSH, to nearby Moorfields Eye Hospital, Europe's oldest and largest centre for ophthalmic treatment, teaching and research. Before attempting a craniotomy, it is important for GOSH to appraise every aspect of Millie's symptoms. You don't want to rush into opening up a child's head without first undertaking a meticulous investigation and assessing all options.

The Moorfields' ophthalmologist confirmed that Millie suffered from optic nerve compression. This was greater in the right eye than in the left with what appeared to be very little or no perception of light in the right eye and 6/60 in the left. In more simplistic terms, the ophthalmologist confirmed she was, almost certainly, irreversibly blind in the right eye and could see at six meters what someone with standard vision could see from sixty meters away. The visible end of her optic nerves, the ones attached to the back of the retina, were pale and almost white. These are normally coloured orange to pink and discoloration is often a sign that nerves are dying or dead as a result of restricted blood flow.

On the short taxi ride back from Moorfields to GOSH, the walls of shadow that had started to rise within me the previous day draw ever closer – it is the loneliest, most scared, most confused I have ever felt as a person, as a husband, as a father. I don't have to ask Vanessa to understand that she too is unable to make sense of it all. Millie is quiet. Subdued. If I was scared, God only knows how she must have felt.

Receiving a confirmatory diagnosis of Millie's likely blindness was tough. As the day unfolded, it was equally tough not knowing whether anything could be done to make her better or at least to reverse the loss of vision. Every minute ticking away meant more and more optic neurons dying and a weakening of her prospects for an improved prognosis. She had a brain tumour, and if that wasn't enough, it was now very likely that, whatever was left of her life would be lived in darkness, the night permanently fastening itself to the very core of her being.

Back in the quiet room, Mr J continues to set out options. He looks between us and the screen that projects the latest MRI of Millie's brain, with a large, opaque, dense, orb-like shape the size of a golf ball in the middle of it. He explains: 'We can operate, as soon as possible. We all have acute concerns over further loss of vision. If we try and debulk the tumour – and by that, I mean reduce its volume as much as possible without damaging the healthy tissue – she may retain what sight she has. Possibly show a slight improvement. Nothing is certain at this stage. We may not even be able to access the tumour. We'll have to assess as we make our way towards it, a millimetre at a time. But we all feel it's worth a try. Worth the risks.'

It occurs to me that it's the first time I have seen Millie's tumour on a screen. I can see the contour of her skull, in profile, and her brain, or at least the outlines of it. The outer cortex, weaving its way inwards and outwards. It is like looking into her essence. It is strange to see her brain projected in this way while looking at Millie in the flesh next to us, being distracted from the screen by a nurse. Too young to understand, too blind to see what was in front of us.

Yesterday morning, I was counting fingers on the sofa with her, not quite knowing what she meant by "fuzzy". A day later we are here, in one of the "quiet rooms" in Koala Ward, staring into Millie's very depths, which now have a small, lumpy shape in the middle, and contemplating the vast expanse of a very uncertain future.

It feels so unreal, so dreamlike in quality. I am thinking like little children think and hoping the power of my thoughts can reverse the narrative. Or make Millie's tumour disappear. Or swap me in her place so that she doesn't have to suffer. I want to change the outcome, but I know I am powerless and completely out of my depth; I know I am not here by choice. I sense the nature of choice itself is going to take on a somewhat ineluctable quality going forward, and I am only going to be left with the illusion of it. An illusion carefully created by the medical professionals around me, or my own self-serving bias, as a means to cope. Or perhaps a bit of both.

The neurosurgeon believes that operating is unequivocally the right thing to do, but the decision, ultimately, lies with Vanessa and me, as Millie's parents, since we must give our consent. That's probably more accurate. I think parents may, in the "fell clutch of circumstance"[14], in the course of traumatic events over which they have no control, confuse the two. They want to feel in control of a situation over which they have no control, in circumstances where their knowledge falls woefully short of that required to make the necessary clinical decisions.

Most of us are, anyway, deluded about the degree to which we understand the world, even in its simplest form. Ask anyone to explain how a basic refrigerator works, let alone a craniotomy, or how to proceed, clinically, when facing our current predicament. It is better to take an honest approach and quickly accept that we have no idea, rather than asking Dr Google to find "the idiot's guide to curing brain cancer" and hope for some useful and valuable insights.

Trusting the experts at GOSH for the big decisions – and trusting orthodox, modern medicine – was the best thing we could have done to improve our daughter's chances of survival at the time.

About a year and a half after Millie finished treatment, I remember taking an interest in a high-profile case involving a five-year-old boy diagnosed with a malignant brain tumour called a medulloblastoma. Medulloblastomas require surgery, often followed by chemotherapy, depending on the age of the child and then, finally, radiotherapy. In this case, aside from his story being perfect tabloid fodder and receiving wide coverage (of the wrong kind, in my view), his parents and the hospital where he was being treated disagreed over his treatment. The hospital argued for conventional radiotherapy whereas the parents *felt* the application of proton beam radiotherapy would provide him with a greater chance for a cure. They seized their son, mid-treatment, to take him abroad.

These parents (neither of whom had paediatric backgrounds) had done their own research. They disagreed with a multidisciplinary team of professionals who provided expert clinical opinion based on years of specialist literature and clinical practice, and not just their own but the cumulative knowledge and practice of all previous consultants. Being a loving parent is not enough to make the right decision for your child. Acting on *feelings* is not a responsible way to behave. One thinks of paving roads and hell and good intentions.

This boy wasn't terminally ill in the strictest sense, but he did have a very serious affliction, with a survival rate of seventy per cent to eighty per cent. So, proton beam was not a last-ditch attempt to save his life, as many headlines suggested at the time.

In our case, while we had to make difficult choices when Millie was undergoing treatment, there was seldom any disagreement on the application of the therapy itself. Thankfully, even though we went through a challenging time, we never found ourselves at the crossroads of life and death decisions. I say thankfully because as parents, we are often ill-equipped to make a balanced judgement in such cases.

Not every clinical decision when curing cancer yields a right or wrong outcome. Differences in outcomes are often subtle. This was certainly true for Millie, who followed a conventional protocol. Although the treatment was tough on her – emotionally, physically, physiologically – the outcomes of each decision, at each stage, more or less followed the multidisciplinary team's predictions.

I am grateful we did not have to make decisions that required letting life – or death – take its course. Especially as such last-ditch attempts often come at considerable cost and suffering to the child. I feel that parents' "I would never forgive myself" argument tends to be deeply, albeit unintentionally, self-centred rather than prioritising the child's best interest. I have seen this first-hand while Millie was undergoing treatment at GOSH. I have known of little boys and little girls who underwent the most corrosive therapies because of their parents' misguided desperation to never give up. Our evolutionary drive to protect our young at all cost misfires in these circumstances. Their lives were extended for a few months, in one case for four years, but at what human cost and to whom?

Adding to the complexity of the decision-making process for Vanessa and me at GOSH was our awareness that young children often lack the competence to make decisions about their treatment. Such responsibility seems to fall to their parents although this is, again, a complete illusion since, unless they have a deep specialism in paediatric oncology or radiation oncology, they will lack the competence to make such judgements. I know I did, but I always felt at GOSH that I could rely on the guidance and advice of the multidisciplinary team looking after my daughter.

On this particular occasion, the team wanted to operate as a matter of urgency. They hoped that the tumour would be accessible and that debulking it might decompress the optic nerve, allow it to breathe a little easier and enable light to travel down its delicate fibres more freely.

The operation was to take place within twenty-four hours, on a Sunday, and GOSH would have to mobilise an entire team to open the second operating theatre used for these types of interventions (usually only one is open on a Sunday). So, we didn't know for certain whether or not it would take place, but the hospital, and Mr J, were trying their utmost.

Before any operation of this kind, the lead neurosurgeon goes through a consent form with the parents and sets candid expectations about possible outcomes, the "it's not my fault if it goes wrong, guv" of every hospital. But the purpose of this, for us, was also to make sure we had no illusions about the seriousness of what was about to happen. That the operation was a risky one, that it could leave Millie blind, or dead, or with life-altering complications as a result of this intervention – not the cancer.

Expectation-setting right at the start of something as complex as treating a child with brain cancer is important for other reasons too: communication with parents, establishing trust and building rapport. We're in it for the long-haul, and it's important the hospital facilitates an environment of openness and honesty, where parents feel they are listened to. As far as our own experience is concerned, GOSH always scored well in this area, especially during the acute phase of treatment when it mattered most. The vast majority of medical professionals took time to ensure we understood the rationale for treatment and what to expect from it: the duration of therapy, its side effects, likely outcomes, what would happen after the operation, how long Millie would be in the intensive care unit. Equally important is providing parents with information a little at a time, almost on a need-to-know basis, so as not to confuse them with the complexity of such an astronomically unfamiliar situation.

Important for us was also the need to be given clear explanations about Millie's condition which made us feel part of the process. Additionally, the doctors, the registrars, and the nurses in particular, showed us compassion and care on a scale we had never experienced before.

The most senior physicians, like Mr J, were always honest about what they knew, and didn't know, about what they could and could not predict, about the severity of the situation, about the likelihood of things going wrong and their possible consequences.

I still have the consent form, a one-page document dated 6 April 2013, that I signed before that first operation. It's a reminder of the time we were confronted with potential loss and, concurrently (the two are connected), the time when we gained an awareness and a better understanding of what it is to be human, to experience love, to appreciate life and to contemplate the finality of death.

The form was filled out by the hand that would open up my daughter's skull later that morning during a procedure described as a "bi-coronal, subfrontal craniotomy and debulking of suprasellar abnormality". *Abnormality...* even physicians can't help but engage in apologetic euphemisms and can't call a brain tumour a brain tumour. It lists other proposed procedures that will be undertaken during the anaesthetic (in Millie's case, the insertion of a catheter), and under the "statement of health professional", it lists the intended benefit and the "serious and frequently occurring risks".

The intended benefit (grand words at this stage, but I'm holding onto those that are thrown at me) is vision preservation. Preservation. That word again. Amongst other benefits will be the taking of a histological sample (for a more formal diagnosis of the tumour) and decompressing the mass, if possible.

The risks – serious and frequently occurring – take a while to sink in. They include various functional impairments to vision, motor and speech, depending on possible damage to cranial nerves (known as cranial nerve palsy), stroke, loss of vision and loss of life.

*

Over the last couple of days, we tried, using age-appropriate language, to keep Millie informed about what was happening to her. I don't know how much of that helped alleviate the fear she must have felt. I take some comfort in thinking that her age may have sheltered her from some of her condition's more sinister aspects, from the gravity of a craniotomy to the very tangible and very material risks associated with it. Not to mention brain cancer, chemotherapy, not recovering her vision and the possibility of dying.

Although she was too young to remember it, I have frequently reminded her, during our walks, about the exceptional way in which she conducted herself – and continues to do so – in facing the hardship of a brain cancer diagnosis. I have no doubt she will eventually appreciate her own immense sense of pride when she finally grasps the strength of character, courage and mental fortitude she demonstrated the morning of her craniotomy and in every minute of every day since then.

I have often relied on her courage to sustain the physical and emotional effort I required. Like the moment I carried her down to theatre for this first brain operation where surgeons would make an incision from one ear to the other, about half an inch from the start of her hairline. Her scalp would be pulled back across her face to expose her forehead, and the surgeon would cut out a small window of bone, by drilling four holes, one in each corner of the window. He would then join the holes by dragging the drill along the sides, exposing her brain and allowing him to make his way, using precision equipment, towards the tumour's bulk.

I would carry her on that short journey without knowing if I would be able to hold her in my arms again later that day. If she would come back as herself, as some altered version, or not at all. Or if I would ever again be able to feel the warmth of her body next to mine, the soft smell of her hair, see her smile, hear her laugh and watch her grow.

I had to dig deep to say, "see you later", as I placed her gently on the operating table, smiling warmly and only scarcely believing it was going to be the case.

When I kissed her forehead, possibly for the last time, as she lay peacefully sleeping after the anaesthetic tipped her into unconsciousness, I drew upon resources I never knew I had to hide the very possible finality of this event.

An intense sadness took hold, sealed with that kiss, that has never really left me. My only consolation is that Millie probably won't ever remember any of it, neither the operation nor that she woke up completely blind, almost nine hours after she was admitted to theatre.

PART TWO
SUMMER

THEMES

Dealing with a shattered future. Children's outlook during and after treatment. Being newbies. How children cope with therapy. How to cope with this total disease. Feeling helpless. Telling children the truth. Understanding chemotherapy. Evaluating long-term side effects.

Summer is only the unfulfilled promise of a spring,
a charlatan in place of the warm and balmy nights I
dream of in April.

THIS SIDE OF PARADISE
F SCOTT FITZGERALD

FROM CAREFREE PAST TO
CARE-FILLED FUTURE

Bedgebury's calm, easy-going summer landscapes often provided some relief from the lingering anxiety which followed the long convalescence following Millie's cancer treatment. During our walks she and I have often spotted flowers and wildlife with delight. On one particularly warm summer's morning, we decided to make our way under the canopy, shielded from the sun, feeling the moist air delicately brush our skin. In the shade of the undergrowth, enchanter's nightshades were in full bloom. These plants are often seen as a nuisance by gardeners but in their natural habitat, these delicate white flowers rose above the unassuming leaves to form a wide cluster of light, star-like splashes against the full green background of their expansive foliage.

I have often wondered if Millie and I contemplated nature in different ways during our walks. Did she just see flowers? Or did this woodland "milky way" evoke in her a sense of our own insignificance in the broader aspects of our existence; a reminder perhaps that we should not let our past dictate our future, that we should not overly worry about what might be coming for us down the line, that we should not try too hard to predict whatever obstacles or challenges we may encounter because of what happened to us yesterday, a week ago, a year ago or in the summer of 2013.

When I peer into the future, it feels different to me than my own contemplations on the past, when I think about my life at any given time. Especially in the big moments, the ones that matter, when the meaning of suffering has found a voice unfamiliar till then.

The future, rather than the past, seems to have, generally, a more granular, distinct character to it. When I imagine my life in the longer term, I can easily picture myself doing this or that, working in this company or another, in this job or that. The expected outcomes seem tangible, distinct, with the alternatives well-defined depending on the option I am inclined to select.

Looking back, the past seems more fluid, its quality somehow more blended and contemplative. There are fewer boundaries and more merging of all the things that have happened to me over the years. The person I am today is a fusion of all the events I have lived through, the cumulative passage of time, the collective gathering of knowledge and experience, the wistful regrets of opportunities I was not willing to seize, or did not recognise as such, of the girls that I did not allow myself to love. The past is a composite. The future is more distinct, more coarse-grained, more individualistic.

The past is often reflective, sometimes regretful. Could I have been something else? Somewhere else? Have I pushed hard enough against the many aborted attempts to take my turmoil in other directions? Or did chance mostly steer the course of my life, in many cases – bar an obvious one – in not too bad a fashion?

The future resembles one of the paths Millie and I take during our frequent strolls. Our focus is progression, deciding a route while experiencing the present of our ongoing conversations, with the rest of life going by, in its endless forms, elsewhere, in the woods and the ponds and the grass.

A second difference between past and future, for me at least, relates to experience. How events can alter the person you are and force you to walk down paths you never thought you'd have to contemplate, changing who the future "you" will be further down the line, as if we become different people depending on which fork in the road we take, often by chance.

That first brain operation was one such instance for me, an event which massively disrupted my possible tomorrows. One day, I was a husband and a father, contemplating a regular, if somewhat privileged, outlook. And the next, I was the father of a girl with brain cancer, who would have to undergo the roughest of treatments and come out on the other side, at best, as a different version of herself. I would have to live through it and accept the consequences of her suffering and exposure to the harshest of maladies. She would likely become someone else entirely. I would likely be left to contemplate a very different future – mine, hers, my family's – to the one I had been building inside my head over the years.

For Millie, experiencing cancer wasn't the only transforming factor at play. Hers was cancer of the organ that most defines us as human beings at all levels: the brain, the command centre for our nervous system. It receives signals from the body's sensory organs and provides information to the muscles. It enables us to think, to feel, to tweet (some say the brain isn't required for that), to laugh, to cry, to walk, to love. To suffer.

Both the illness and the treatment were going to alter her – irreversibly, irrevocably – emotionally, physically, hormonally, physiologically. It is a matter of fact that Millie has become a different person to who she would have been. The only questions that the medical professionals were unable to answer during treatment were, "by how much" and "over what period of time"? and whether or not all this, in the long-term, really matters.

Millie often ponders this existential conundrum as we put one foot in front of the other, smelling the air, contemplating a long line of silver birches swaying in a warming breeze.

'How has cancer changed me do you think?' she might ask. 'I wonder what I would be like as a person if I hadn't had what I had? I wonder how close I am to the Millie I would have been, or how different?'

'What do you mean by that?' I probe. 'How would this be useful to you now?'

Behind these enquiries is her desire to understand the difference so that she can better deal with some of the disabilities cancer has thrown her way. An example might help here. For physiological reasons I will explain in more detail later in the book, Millie feels hungry (really hungry) all the time. Having insight into "normal" hunger might enable her, she believes, to better manage her appetite. It's as if she needs a "control" Millie who lives in a parallel universe, who hadn't had to go through her ordeal and against whom she could compare and adjust herself. And therein lies the challenge. There is no control environment, no parallel universe, and so no one will ever know.

For parents and carers, I do sense that the notion of a parallel Millie might be helpful, not just to answer her questions but to better support her to maximise her potential and become the best possible version of herself. In the first few years after treatment, as we attempted to close some of the physical, psychological and emotional gaps the cure and cancer had opened up, we faced some practical difficulties in not knowing what her potential might be against what it would have been prior to cancer, what the right benchmark we were trying to reach was. Was she distracted in class because of the medication she was taking? Or was she naturally distracted as a pupil, and would have been anyway, irrespective of her cancer? Not bothered with friendships, she preferred her own company to that of other children her age. Was introspection a natural trait, or had it been emphasised by some of the side effects caused by chemotherapy and radiotherapy?

This was challenging in the early years following the end of treatment because she had fallen so behind her peers, on so many levels. Our focus was on re-establishing some form of normality, to bring her back to a more "normal" version of herself. And whilst we felt it was important to push and encourage, we didn't necessarily want to bark up the wrong tree if, on balance, making friends, for example, was never going to be top of her priority list (it was never top of mine either).

Normality wasn't something Vanessa and I were thinking about as we could no longer assume that Millie could attend school without worrying about missing life-saving medications or that she could follow the curriculum without specialist assistance, have the emotive faculties to make friends, to fall in love, to engage in human relationships and to contemplate the kind of life choices she had before this wretched disease.

We were misguided in our thinking, of course. We were learning ourselves, in a sense, to deal with disability in the right way. We had not yet reconciled, in our own mind, that her life was going to be different, and how she was going to negotiate it was going to be different than the rest of us, using different coping mechanisms, different tools with which to navigate the world around her. Not worse, but different.

And yet suddenly, the mundane routine of life became one of our most desirable outcomes as we waited for Millie to emerge from her first brain operation.

*

At 3:27pm, on Sunday, 7 April 2013, after more than eight agonising hours, Mr J finally appears in reception outside Koala Ward, dressed in his blue scrubs, a head cover and with his mask loose, hanging at the side of his neck.

'It's gone very well; Millie's doing very well and is waking up,' he reassures us quickly. 'We were able to access the site and relieve some of the pressure the tumour was placing on the optic nerves.' We learn that she is in "resus", the "resuscitation" room usually close to the operating theatre where specially trained staff, with specialist medical equipment, monitor patients while they wake up from major surgery.

Mr J also tells us that this is not the type of tumour they had originally thought it was (an astrocytoma) but has the consistency of a craniopharyngioma (although it will eventually turn out not to be this type of tumour either). The histopathology of the sample taken during the operation will confirm what we are dealing with. I have mentioned this before, but it took a good few days to confirm the right diagnosis and the right plan to treat Millie's cancer. For no other reasons than that's how long it normally takes and that cancer is a complex disease.

Mr J would like us to go to resus straight away to help establish if the operation has made any difference to her eyesight.

I feel a strange mixture of panic, apprehension and relief in seeing Millie wriggling on the bed, crying, clearly dazed, spaced out, seemingly looking around her but for nothing in particular. *She's alive!* I tell myself. *That's something.* None of the big risks that were mentioned to us before the operation have materialised.

Her head is bandaged up with white dressing, and tubes are coming out of everywhere, but she still looks like Millie. She is agitated but settles instantly when she hears Vanessa's voice.

Millie asks for some water and Mr J asks us to put the bottle slightly out of reach to establish whether she can see it and if her vision has improved. It hasn't. She can't make anything out. I look up at Mr J who looks doubtful. Despite his heavy-handed pre-op setting of expectations, he was clearly hoping for some improvement. *That's it*, I say to myself. *She's blind*. I make a deliberate effort to park my feelings for now – Millie is the focus.

After a brief spell in resus, she is brought up to the ward's intensive care department – called the High Dependency Unit (just to rub it in?) – a large room, with a bed in each corner and each with its own complicated resuscitation and monitoring equipment.

A nurse is assigned, full-time, to each of the four patients. A nurse for the day and one for the night. They are some of the most extraordinary people I have ever met. I have no doubt that the highly emotional nature of our situation distorted how I felt about them, still, they cared for my daughter and genuinely cared about their job. So, of course, I was going to, quite literally, fall in love with each and every one of them. It was the kind of love you have for your family or that a young, helpless child has for their parents.

I will always remember the enormous capacity for humanity of the nurses, Maria, Vanessa, Chloe and Jesse in particular. They operated as a human buffer between us, laypeople and newbies as far as curing cancer is concerned, and the complex way in which cancer treatment is delivered. This is something that takes time to adjust to.

GOSH is an intricate, specialist medical establishment which treats cancer patients with input from different professionals whose vocational fields I had barely heard of before: neurosurgeons, paediatric oncologists, paediatric radiation oncologists, radiographers, nephrologists, endocrinologists, physiotherapists, ophthalmologists and audiologists. All of whom were consultants involved at stages of Millie's treatment and in managing her cure.

And management is the appropriate word here. Curing cancer, and brain cancer specifically, involves managing a decision-making process and an approach for each individual patient, according to a specific protocol. A cure isn't straightforward but a road with unexpected bends, obstacles and diverging forks that must be carefully navigated.

The letter I mentioned earlier – the one given to us by Millie's lead oncologist, Dr H, a couple of days after this first operation – alludes to this rocky road. It explains that:

The current recommended treatment, which has shown the best results so far, is to treat with four courses of chemotherapy, to assess the radiological response and if significant residual is left, to consider surgical resection prior to focal radiotherapy.

Then, we were entirely unaware of the enormous implications of chemotherapy, radiological response, resection and focal radiotherapy.

Of course, we had discussed these options with Dr H, which he described as: "following several discussions and written information, both Millie and her parents agreed to this management plan and consented to start chemotherapy on 15 April 2013". Let's set aside for now the notion that Millie was able to agree, or that we, as her parents, were able to apply any considered judgement about how to cure her cancer so early on in the process. Or realise what the immediate future would hold or the extraordinary level of energy that would be required to navigate the difficult path over months and months of treatment to remission.

Four courses of chemotherapy meant that Millie would remain, broadly, an inpatient of GOSH for the next four months. It also meant she would lose her hair, suffer from stomach aches, experience pain from possible nerve damage and become immunodeficient, while her fertility, in the long-term, would be compromised, her kidney might suffer irreparable damage and she might lose her hearing. Permanently. And all because of the treatment, not the cancer.

The tumour mass, and whether or not chemotherapy is effective in reducing it, is assessed and monitored using radiology, "the radiological response". This implies that it might, or might not, be effective, which was not worth pondering for now.

"Surgical resection of the residual" (removing whatever remains of the tumour if chemo is successful in shrinking it) means at least one, if not more, brain operations which all carry the same risks: strokes, loss of life, permanent blindness. Something I was not quite mentally equipped to contemplate, having just experienced this operation.

It takes time to adjust to the extreme discomfort of cancer treatment. I was craving the familiar, wishing I could take refuge in my previous life. My deep unconscious was screaming at me, resisting the changes that were happening to us, mourning the loss of who we were before 5 April 2013. It is often the case that, over the course of a lifetime, our expectation is that we should constantly be well or that our loved ones should be. From the time our children are born, we try to evade the thought that they may suffer or become sick at some point in their lives. It takes this type of event to give us a better sense of clarity that suffering can happen to anyone, at any time.

The suffering that cancer imposes on us requires to be addressed appropriately not just at the clinical level. Getting better also relies on our ability to engage with this disease in the right way emotionally. Our relationship with the illness often defines our ability to accept, and eventually to overcome, grief. Coming to terms with life's imperfections, including illnesses, helps us confront moments of crisis with less panic or fear. And that however much Vanessa and I might feel lost at this moment in time, engaging with our pain in the right way eventually allows a smoother transition towards repair. This is something I will return to in the last chapter of this book when looking at grief.

Following chemotherapy and another one, possibly two, brain operations, Millie will undergo "focal radiotherapy" to her head for at least a couple of months. This treatment carries some permanent loss of cognition, further damage to her pituitary and hypothalamus and increases her lifetime risk of secondary malignancies.

Unsurprisingly, decisions on the application of treatment at GOSH are considered by a Multidisciplinary Team (MDT), in Millie's case, led by her oncologist Dr H. At GOSH the MDT meets every Tuesday morning[15] to review the progress and challenges of each case, all before consulting with the patient and in our case, the patient's parents, on these critical decisions. The team also leverages knowledge gathered over years, both nationally and internationally, about best practice guidelines not just for brain cancer but this specific type of brain cancer. All the more reason for parents to resist the temptation of relying on Dr Google.

For suprasellar secreting germ cell tumours, a multimodal treatment is required where chemotherapy tries to shrink the tumour, an operation removes whatever's left and radiotherapy destroys anything "malignant" that either chemo or surgery could not remove.

*

Up until April 2013, I was a scramble of mostly positive experiences, with little appetite for regret or desire to retouch the past. Like most people, I sensed that chance had mostly steered the course of my life, and in my case, it had done so in not too bad a fashion.

Now, our future, once crisp with possibilities, was uncertain, with the practical implications of Millie's long-term disabilities and their magnitude outside of my control. It seems that over the timeframe of a lifetime, pain and difficult choices are just fair payment for the good fortune of being alive. A reminder – in the cruellest possible way – of how little we have charge of what we care about most and that we are seldom the authors of the events that mark us most severely. For the next few months at least, Millie would not be the author of hers.

For now, Vanessa and I were facing a steep and arduous learning curve that we could barely fathom. For, no matter how many consultations we had with specialists in the first few days, no matter how many factsheets we read, no matter how much detail was explained, ultimately, there is no substitute for our experience. As we were quickly finding out, experience is a very harsh and uncompromising teacher. But we learned, my God, we learned.

As the various drips, lines and drains fed back data about Millie's recovery to the beeping and bleeping machines which monitored her vital signs of life, second by second, it dawned on us we were now strangers in the strangest of lands.

A FOREIGN LAND

The first couple of days in the high dependency ward are relatively tranquil for us which, given recent events, was strange. After the cataclysmic disruption to our everyday life, and the confusion over the past two days about Millie's condition, news about her brain tumour, loss of eyesight and what to do about it, we are enveloped in the protective custody of GOSH. The staff have dealt with this type of situation before and take control. While Millie faces something life changing and risky, at least positive action is being taken to reverse the course of the disease and to improve her health.

Millie is stable, on morphine for pain but drifting in and out of sleep. Even when she surfaces, on occasions, she seems mostly sleepy and confused. We are told not to worry, that all the "vital signs" of her pulse, blood pressure, temperature and blood oxygen levels are absolutely fine. She recognises our voices and knows that Vanessa and I are here. It reassures us to know that she knows and this, hopefully, reassures her.

All the soft tissues surrounding her eyes are swollen from the operation. The skin on her forehead was pulled back across her face to access the tumour from the front and this caused some swelling, also very normal. But it means that the nurses and ophthalmologists on their rounds can't check her pupils' reaction to light.

Before the swelling really took hold, there had been some very (very!) faint signs that both her eyes were reacting, a positive signal that the optic nerves were not entirely damaged. We won't know for a while whether this will affect her eyes' functionality or whether the little that seems to remain will be enough for some recovery of functional vision. You don't need one hundred per cent of your optic nerves to be able to clearly see one hundred per cent of the outside world. It isn't a linear relationship. And the younger you are, the better and quicker your brain can adapt to compensate for such weakness.

Being in this highly controlled environment on Koala Ward, with Millie asleep and peaceful, allows me to absorb the events of the past three days. At night, when the lights go out on the ward, sleep comes amidst the murmuring of the monitors, interrupted now and again by beeps that indicate a transfusion has finished, or a pulse has dropped below a certain level. Only one parent can sleep here so I opt to do the first night. Looking around, I recall my first walk through the ward, when I brought the MRI scan from the Portland Hospital the day Millie's eyes went "fuzzy". That was only two days ago, in my other life.

Back then, in a world most unfamiliar, horrifying and spine-chilling to the core, I floated past children recovering from operations to their heads and brains. The detail didn't register.

I didn't notice the faces of parents waiting in the reception room, anxious for their child to emerge from the operating theatre. Nor did I pay much attention to the children in the high dependency ward where equipment monitored their vital signs, as they do for Millie now. I didn't see the drips linked to a canula, a little tube inserted into a vein on her hand, used for frequent blood tests and transfusions of platelets and antibiotics. I had ignored the arterial lines, another tube used to measure arterial pressure and oxygen levels. I was not yet sensitive to the catheters, another tube inserted into the bladder via the urinary tract to measure urine output. In all probability, I subconsciously blocked out the drains that disappeared under dressings on their heads and were inserted to gather blood, tissue fluids and other discharges following surgery.

It didn't occur to me then that Millie would be one of those children. That Vanessa and I would be those parents, heavy with emergent knowledge we never thought we would need. That I would be here, next to Millie, lying on a reclining chair for parents, trying to make sense of the malignant cluster bomb that had been dropped on us a few days back.

It was all so new. Would I be able to cope and to support Millie and my family through this ordeal?

This was my first intimate encounter with this disease. Of course, I had heard of cancer before (who hasn't?), of its possible signs and symptoms, of its related – more or less effective – cures and of the various specialists involved in its alleviation. I had heard of friends' parents being diagnosed and treated. In her more advanced age, my mother had a brush with cancer, albeit a slow growing one and not in the brain, as did both of my father's sisters. But they were all significantly older than either Millie or me, had all survived after receiving treatment which was, compared to my daughter's, relatively mild.

Sitting in Koala Ward, my world turned to black, lost its depth and its vibrancy, which are dimensions that, even over time, never regain their full qualities. Every morning, every sunrise came as a betrayal and a daily reminder that my daughter's life had changed irrevocably.

In that moment, Vanessa and I were experiencing shock, despair, anguish, pain, sadness and hopelessness. We had a deep-seated uncertainty about what each and every unfolding hour would bring, knowing the road ahead would be far from easy for Millie. All of this was compounded by the deep sense of injustice we felt about the rarest of rare diseases materialising in our daughter's brain.

We quickly realised that, for the foreseeable future, each day would bring the heart-wrenching act of holding life and death in balance. Millie's lot, for now, was going to be to suffer and, possibly, to die.

As we were quickly discovering, cancer treatment takes absolute control of your life. As the unfortunate narrative began to unfold in the first few days, it became clear that Millie's condition would not be cured with paracetamol and a good night's sleep. We had to clear our diaries and forget our plans: family holidays, weekends, work, friends, playdates, and meals together.

And yet every parent who has gone through something similar realises the absolute truth that your feelings don't matter. What mattered was Millie and how she felt. What mattered was our ability to cope, to be physically and emotionally available for her when she most needed us. It comes naturally to all parents. There's no credit to be had.

Despite our commitment to be with Millie, the first two weeks were often uncertain and confusing. Vanessa and I felt completely disoriented, as if lost in an alien and hostile environment, without a map, compass or translator. It would take time to adjust to our new surroundings, vocabulary, protocols and tests relating to cancer and its cure.

Despite its harshness, this foreign land is, paradoxically, quite welcoming. Medical institutions such as GOSH, and the resident professionals who would guide us through the complexities of this terrain, were outstanding. We became quickly aware that nurses and paediatric consultants were there on merit, mostly using their heads rather than their hearts. Rational compassion, not empathy, of the most remarkable kind prevails.

The medical language, with its mix of dull and difficult vocabulary and acronyms galore, takes some adjustment. I had seldom encountered words such as suprasellar secreting germ cell tumour, cisplatin, etoposide, ifosfamide, PIE (pronounced like the "pie" in "apple pie"), G-CSF, GFR, alphafetoprotein, beta-hCG, cytology and double lumen Hickman line. All these were words casually included in that very first letter received from GOSH.

Nor had I ever been exposed to the multitude of rituals and tests associated with this type of disease. For an illness that mostly grows from the inside out, it is regrettable that the cure usually requires access from the outside in. It took some time to acclimatise to the frequent blood tests, cerebrospinal fluid extractions, glomerular filtration rate assessments (GFRs – kidney function tests) and central venous catheter insertions, to name but a few.

This unfamiliar territory, so all-encompassing to begin with, is a place that brain cancer patients especially, and their families, seldom leave. Passports are revoked on entry and stamped with the burden of a multitude of side effects – often life-altering and permanent – caused by the disease and its devastating cure.

As I contemplated this grave new world, during the nights following Millie's first brain operation, occasionally glancing at her, slow breathing as she lay next to me, I realised that the end of cancer treatment marks the beginning of a new life.

It would probably not be the life we had before. Possibly not a worse life, though it certainly seemed that way at that moment in time, or a better life, come to think of it. But it would be a different life, spent managing the aftermath of cancer and its associated therapies.

That is the harsh reality of brain cancer – there is no easy way to live through it. Eventually, if treatment is successful, one must become accustomed to a new kind of normal.

For parents, deep anxiety is just one price they pay for the possibility of a cancer-free future. But for Millie, the little memory she has of cancer and its treatment is not coloured with confusion, or with the colossal sense of injustice my wife and I felt at the time.

Her thoughts, feelings, especially fears, were more pedestrian and functional, as they tend to be in children who often live much more in the moment. "Can I bring my comfort blanket to the operating theatre when they put me to sleep before my brain operation?", "am I allowed popcorn in the high dependency ward?", "will it be the same nurse looking after me tomorrow night?"

This seems to be the case for most survivors I've spoken to and when the age of diagnosis is close to Millie's. But even those who underwent treatment as late as thirteen years of age barely remember their time in hospital. Research in this field often suggests that treatment intensity is not associated with poor psychological outcomes[16]. Children seem better equipped, emotionally and physically, to adapt to clinical trauma. This might be cold comfort, but I am inclined to take it since, on this harshest of journeys, you take what you can.

As a result of cancer and its treatment, Millie would become a Millie without youthful energy, without drive, without spark, without the ability to produce hormones, without full faculty to retain information in her short-term memory, without a normal processing speed, without the emotional know-how to reconnect with the friends she had before treatment, or her very own sister and brother, without the ability to establish new friendships, without a hunger stopcock to tell her brain when her gut was full, without the awareness to stop eating incessantly as if possessed by gluttony personified, without any prospect of living a life free of daily medications.

And yet, as I often reminded myself in my low moments, she was still a Millie with a prospect of some sort of life, with love in her heart, with loving parents by her side and a brother and a sister who would play a crucial part in her recovery. A young girl with her own hopes and aspirations, with a strength and a desire to get better, with a yearning to return to the life she had left behind.

She wouldn't be alone in navigating these upslopes. I knew then, as I know now, that Vanessa and I would be there at every step of her slow, arduous ascent.

*

Right from the start of our time at GOSH, we realised that cancer would take absolute control of our lives. We would become immersed in its treatment and surveillance, captive in a world we did not fully understand. As we discovered, cancer isn't just one disease but many, each with its specific treatment and protocol. The nature of the disease and the way in which cure is applied would, literally, obliterate Millie and take her to the brink of death several times over.

And yet, everyone at GOSH made it very clear that children were, in fact, far more resilient than adults when undergoing cancer treatment. And their outcomes frequently more positive.

'Children are amazing,' the nurses would say. 'One day you think they will never recover, and the next day, they're walking about and playing in the playroom.' Although these observations didn't provide any immediate comfort, after just two days Millie had recovered enough that some of the monitoring apparatus could be removed, and she moved into a single room with less medical supervision.

Over the previous six months or so pre-diagnosis, Millie's bedtime routine began to include a gentle back rub whilst listening to "From Here to the Moon and Back" sung by Dolly Parton. I guess she found it as soothing as I did. I loved this moment and perhaps subconsciously wished to prolong it, sensing harder times ahead.

During this time, as signs of life resurfaced, and the combination of pain-relieving post-operative drugs wore off, Millie started listening to her iTouch and her favourite song. Although her eyes were still swollen, she could lip-sync the words in her darkness. Even now, as I recall the lyrics and melody of the song while writing this, I can feel my tears welling up.

We still didn't really know what she was thinking, but we would talk to her all the time. We would tell her she would get better, that feeling rotten after such a big operation is normal, that the swelling around her eyes would subside, that she would be able to open them again soon, and before long, all of this would be behind us. How do you even begin a conversation with a seven-year-old about the prospect of never regaining her vision?

We hoped the nurses and doctors were right about children being amazing, about their potential for recovery, about their greater resilience to the onslaught of cancer treatment, about how cancer in children is more responsive to treatment than in adults. How much truth was there in those assertions or were they served up to soften the blow of what would lie ahead? How much of it represented a fair and impartial assessment of reality?

CONSENTING TO TREATMENT

'We'd like to start chemotherapy as soon as Millie has recovered sufficiently from her operation,' explains Dr H.

I am familiar with the term "chemotherapy" but am not exactly prepared for it in the context of my daughter's cancer. Millie will have chemotherapy, and in less than a week! Eight days after her first brain operation. The fast pace of her cancer treatment is something else that hasn't quite sunk in over these first few hellish days. Just as Dr H's words linger without their meaning fully forming, my brain rejecting them, my every synaptic connection is unwilling to commit this to memory, averse to translating it into something I am experiencing now. I can't properly understand what all of this will mean for Millie.

'We're currently looking at the week beginning 15 April,' continues Dr. H. 'The protocol for her type of cancer is four courses of chemotherapy over approximately four months, called PIE protocol. We will reassess her tumour after two courses, including a repeat CSF for tumour markers and cytology.'

PIE? CSF? Cytology? More terminology to learn. Dr H would eventually unpack for us what all of this would mean in practice. This first consultation about chemotherapy was the beginning of our education about what cancer is (and isn't) and how different it all turns out to be when children have it.

Firstly, brain cancer as an illness is a total disease. It had wrapped itself around Millie like a permanent heavy cloak, physically, neurologically, emotionally, socially, physiologically and hormonally. It would envelop her during treatment and thereafter.

Partly, this is because many paediatric cancer treatments must be immediate and sustained. Like Millie's, many childhood cancers are only discovered in the later stages when the chance of it having spread to other organs and tissues is higher. The "CSF" Dr H mentioned stands for cerebrospinal fluid which we've discussed earlier. And GOSH had already extracted a sample for "cytology" during her first brain operation. So far, there were no signs that her cancer had advanced to other parts of the body. We weren't home and dry, however, because sometimes there aren't enough cancer-affected cells for cytology to detect their presence, and repeat checks are required at key stages of treatment.

The other consequence of childhood cancers being discovered at a late stage is that treatment is generally more intensive than it is for adult cancers. Children can often handle higher doses of chemotherapy drugs before serious side effects occur since their bodies, we are told, are more resilient. They are more efficient and better able to recover from surgery, as well as filtering out infusions of drugs and toxic chemicals. Higher doses can enable more effective treatment, which is generally the case in childhood cancers.

Childhood cancers are different too because, unlike those found in adults, they do not result from lifestyle choices, such as poor diet or smoking. They may also be different at the cellular, molecular level. Something both outside the scope of this book and my own knowledge.

The stage of disease progression, the need to respond with urgency and the fact that children can sustain more intense treatment often results in therapy at a very high pace. This presents challenges for parents, and it certainly did for us.

Consider, for example, Millie's timeline, paying particular attention to the dates. She was admitted to GOSH as an emergency case on 6 April 2013. Seven months after her initial diagnosis, on 2 November, she had undergone three brain operations: on 7 April, two months later on 5 June and her last one on 27 August.

Shortly after her first operation, she had an additional procedure under general anaesthetic to insert a Hickman line, a central venous catheter, to administer drugs over four cycles of chemotherapy. This was a double tube going into the side of her chest and then into one of the main veins feeding the heart. It would remain in place for much longer than the duration of the cure.

She underwent two cycles of chemotherapy either side of her second craniotomy, in April, May, June and July. Each cycle of chemo lasted approximately ten days as an inpatient, with twenty days at home (with frequent day visits to the local hospital for monitoring) to allow the body to recover from the toxic onslaught. Eleven days after her last operation, and following the end of chemotherapy, on 8 September 2013, we flew to Oklahoma City where

Millie went through thirty daily sessions of proton beam radiotherapy over the course of two months. The treatment and location were only confirmed six days before we left.

Between April and November that year, Millie received more than two dozen blood and platelet transfusions, seventy-odd blood tests, twelve MRI scans (not counting the thirty scans undertaken to line up the beam of protons prior to administering her dose of daily radiation), nine tomography evaluations of her retina, litres and litres of antibiotics, gallons of toxic chemicals injected into her body and other tests to monitor the performance and health of organs such as her kidneys, her ovaries and her ears affected by the various therapies.

This level of commitment to Millie and GOSH required us to plan carefully. We couldn't just press the pause button on the rest of our lives. Ellie and Luca needed to go to school; bills needed to be paid and work engagements managed.

Childhood cancer doesn't just affect children. Millie was our absolute focus, but her circle of friends and family wasn't restricted just to Vanessa and me. Her sister and brother were undoubtedly going to require emotional support. Our extended family, our own respective parents, Millie's grandparents, were also going to be negatively impacted alongside cousins, teachers, schoolmates, friends, as well as our work colleagues and clients. In that sense, a child's circle of family and friends may be larger and require even more emotional resources than it does for adults.

Making people aware of Millie's condition, however, was easier than I imagined. Her cancer became a yardstick against which I started measuring my own life's problems and those of others. Rightly or wrongly, it very quickly recalibrated my compass about what was and wasn't important. Compared to what I was seeing her go through, and the prospect of several difficult months in hospital, telling family and friends seemed trivial at best.

Equally, I was aware that those closest to us would be upset by the news of her illness, and I wanted to be sensitive to their feelings. For my own parents, in particular, who were older than Vanessa's parents, and lived in Italy, the news would take its toll since I was their son, and they could offer little practical support. They would feel my pain in the most visceral, helpless sense just as I was feeling it for Millie.

Vanessa's family were more willing and better equipped to help. They lived close by, so for the initial few days post-diagnosis at least, Ellie and Luca could stay with their grandmother and aunt and cousins.

Millie's siblings knew what Mummy and Daddy and Millie were up to, that she was in hospital, she was going to have an operation to make her eyes better and she was going to stay to make her condition better. For now, that's all they needed to know. The harder conversations, especially with my eldest, Ellie, nine at the time, would come later.

Keeping Millie updated, however, couldn't wait. Informing one's child of their cancer is vastly different to informing an adult. How much and how little she should know, given her age, was difficult to gauge, and GOSH provided very little guidance. Every child is different; every seven-year-old is different. We would have to rely on our instincts as parents, on our knowledge of Millie as a person.

Compounding the desolation I felt then was a deep sense of helplessness and inadequacy – for the first time in my life I could not make it better for Millie. I was no longer in control of her well-being. At least in the short term, I would have to radically redefine my role as her father.

Understanding this quickly felt like an important and critical step in surviving the brutal pace of treatment during these first two weeks. It's one every parent of a child with cancer will recognise. My new responsibility, more than ever before, was going to be that of translator, guide and custodian of Millie's well-being. She would depend on me, and on my wife, for helpful, accurate and truthful information, for ensuring we understood what was happening, to the best of our abilities, and relaying it in the most appropriate way.

During treatment at least, our duty was to help her deal with the painful therapies that lay ahead, ensuring that she had some comprehension of them and some control over her situation. That she felt safe. And we would need to support the medics in complying with and applying treatment protocols over many months.

There were several elements here: making decisions about treatment, and then which aspects of these, and the possible outcomes of her condition, to share with Millie.

We would make decisions about her care guided by information and advice from physicians, commonly referred to as informed consent. Millie was under the age of sixteen so did not have the legal right (or know-how or judgment) to make her own decisions about treatment so could not provide consent[17]. This added another subtle dimension to her treatment.

The risks of treating childhood brain cancer are significant. We were asked to make decisions that would affect the very fabric and quality of her future life. It is one thing for an adult to agree to a cure that will make her infertile, as the chemo Millie would receive was predicted to do, and quite another to agree for one of the three human beings you love the most in the entire planet to be submitted to it.

GOSH did consult with us; they explained and gave us factsheets, but I was aware that the devastating news that Millie had cancer could well compromise my ability to make informed, objective judgements. In particular when the clinical urgency added pressure. We were in a state of shock for much of the first two weeks. It's possible that GOSH understands and manages this without parents being fully aware. I hope so.

Regardless, I always felt strongly that she deserved the truth. She was the one suffering, the one who needed to prepare herself for what was to come, the one who needed to adjust to a different life in the aftermath of the diagnosis.

I didn't want to deprive Millie of the opportunity to make her own choices. These were restricted, as they were for us, but she needed some control, even an illusion of it. So, it became important for Millie to decide when to eat, when to drink, when to go to the toilet, when to go to the playroom, when to rest, when to be read to and when to listen to music.

I wanted to equip her with some knowledge of what was to come, without colouring her outlook. I clearly felt some tension between being honest and the responsibility to protect her, given her age, and her inability to fully appraise the situation.

Equally, there was no point in lying to her. Millie knew this was out of the ordinary. She knew, despite our best efforts to conceal it, what the look on our faces meant when brain cancer was first uttered or craniotomy initially articulated. The needles and the doctors and the scanners were real. It comes naturally to all of us to trust our experience. We all grow up doing so, consciously or otherwise. I did not see the point in being evasive.

But I could also appreciate that truth can take more than one form in our situation. The truth that would exist for Millie, now and in the future, was going to be different to the sense of loss Vanessa and I were feeling. We had our own ideas about what Millie would be giving up as a result of her condition or knowing more about it. Millie was not thinking the way we were. And I kept repeating that to myself, trying to assuage my own immense anxiety about having to be frank with her.

Being true, I decided, would be central to how we would live through the next seven months and our lives beyond that. We were going to tell the truth as we believed it to be. Consultants at GOSH did it with us all the time. They would never say "we're hopeful she'll recover her eyesight". Instead, a medic might say "she may recover some of her eyesight. Some children have surprised us in the past. Others don't do so well. I can't tell you exactly what will happen with Millie, but both her eyes are reactive to light, and this is usually a good sign. But we'll have to wait and see if it will have an effect on her vision from a functional perspective".

Yes. We needed to tell the truth as we believed it to be.

And so, we promised Millie the day before her first operation: 'This is not going to be easy,' we said. 'You are not going to understand everything that's going to happen to you over the next few weeks. To be honest, it will also be difficult for Mummy and Daddy to understand everything. And we're not going to have answers for everything you want to know either. But we promise you that we will tell you the truth as we believe it to be. Even if it's really difficult to hear. Even if we know it will be upsetting. Because we feel you deserve to know what is happening and that we will help you bear it. Are you okay with that, Millie?'

I have often wondered if this was the right approach and if we made the right decision. After all, parents think nothing of lying to their children about Father Christmas, the tooth fairy, that "we're almost there" on a journey when we're not even close, or about the farm their favourite pet moved to for a happier life.

But this was different. Ultimately, I wanted her to feel supremely confident in this environment, however hard, that I would not and could not lie to her about anything related to her cancer or its cure.

And Millie, though we weren't sure at this stage, would inhabit this planet for many years to come. I wanted an older Millie to feel I had behaved in the right way. That I had not been deceitful, even in good faith, to shield her from information of which she was the rightful owner.

I have often brought the topic up myself during our walks. Questions weren't just one-directional. I could also ask them and probe her point of view. Strolling along a collection of yews, careful to avoid the red, sticky, fleshy berries dispersed on the path, I would say, 'Do you know how we always told you we were going to tell you the truth during your treatment and afterwards? No matter how hard it was to hear it? Would you have preferred it if we had protected you a little bit more? Perhaps, keeping some of the more difficult things to ourselves?'

Her answers were always unequivocal. She wanted to know. 'It was annoying to hear things, but I understood they were needed and for a good cause. To help me get better,' she would declare. She felt it prepared her better for the test, or the needle, or the operation that was about to come. 'I could take the tears out of it. If I had time to ready myself mentally, I felt I could face injections and operations without getting too upset.'

Still, adopting a philosophy and implementing it are very different propositions. Familiarity, in this instance, has never bred contempt. And time, practice and experience have never made those conversations any easier.

And whilst it may have been right to aspire to have honest conversations with Millie, it was quite another to have them. How do you even begin to muster the courage to say to your seven-year-old daughter: 'You will have a brain operation, Millie. But we don't know for certain if it will fix your eyes.' Or, 'The doctors will start giving you strong medicines to shrink the bad cells in your brain. Unfortunately, the strong medicines will make you feel lousy; you'll have to spend the next four months in hospital; and it will make all your soft, beautiful hair fall out.'

PREPARING FOR CHEMOTHERAPY

If any of us are asked to name the treatment most associated with curing cancer, most of us would say chemotherapy. That's what I would have said before all of this started, without realising I knew very little about it until it was administered to Millie.

As an option for curing cancer, it is less than seventy years old. It was discovered by chance during the First World War when scientists found that soldiers exposed to poisonous chemical warfare, such as mustard gas, had depleted bone marrow cells and lymph nodes.

Further research, during and after the Second World War, refined and changed the chemical compound and its dose delivery so that it could be used in trials to treat, initially, lymphomas, a rare type of blood cancer affecting lymphocytes, cells that specialise in fighting infections. This particular chemical, or chemotherapy "agent", served as a model for the development of further agents treating other types of cancers over the next decades. Most worked on the key principles of chemotherapy, namely, to kill fast replicating cells, like cancer cells – while sparing replicating normal cells – by damaging their DNA, interfering with cell division or disrupting their ability to replicate. Or a little bit of all those together. And then hitting them again before they have time to recover, which is why chemotherapy often comes in multiple "cycles".

After the initial trials, it took time to develop agents that were effective against particular cancers, whilst agent combination trials attempted to reduce the risk of cancer cell resistance to a single agent. Using more than one agent at a time became known, unsurprisingly, as combination chemotherapy and proved more successful, although more toxic, than using one chemical at a time. Waves and waves of new chemotherapy drugs have been developed over the last four decades from a variety of sources, including plant extracts, heavy metal compounds and antibiotics.

Treating patients with chemotherapy has become more scientific and targeted over the years and in particular over the last three decades with the introduction of clinical trials. This has enabled the comparison of treatments to improve efficacy against all types of cancer. What's more, and thankfully for Millie, drugs to reduce temporary side effects of chemotherapy, such as nausea, vomiting and intensive support care, have also improved.

In its current form, chemotherapy consists of, in the main, an injection of cytotoxic (meaning toxic to living cells) chemicals directly into the bloodstream[18]. These substances can destroy the very core of cellular structures, and combining agents is analogous to mixing a poisonous cocktail with devastating effects on the body. The degree is dependent on which agents, since some are more toxic than others, and the dose given to patients. The greater the dose, the greater the efficacy but also the greater the potential for damage to healthy tissues and organs.

Of all the things I knew about chemotherapy before Dr H outlined Millie's protocol, its long-term damage to other organs of the body wasn't one of them. And this is irrespective of how often your paediatric oncologist explains it or how many times you read the simplistic factsheets on therapy given to parents before treatment starts.

Merely a week after her first brain operation, Dr H takes Vanessa and me aside to discuss the plan for the next few months. 'We're looking to start chemotherapy on Monday or Tuesday next week, with PIE protocol,' he says. 'We're planning to administer four courses over four months and reassess with an MRI scan and measurement of tumour markers after two courses. So, halfway through.' PIE, he says, is the mix of chemicals which will be injected into Millie's bloodstream over the next few months. Each letter stands for the specific agent used.

P is for Cisplatin, and probably the most corrosive of the three compounds which will be used. It is the generic name given to a trade name drug called Platinol (hence the P), a nasty, heavy-metal-based alkylating agent. Alkylating agents are one of the drugs used against cancer, some – though not cisplatin – direct descendants of mustard gases used in chemical warfare. We don't need to worry ourselves with the molecular differences between agents here, and there are many other classes such as plant alkaloids, antitumour antibiotics, topoisomerase inhibitors. It's complicated and beyond my understanding, but you get the picture.

Cisplatin, the medics tell us rather matter-of-factly, is associated with higher risks of quite significant long-term damage to Millie's hearing and kidneys. GOSH's literature, which talks about *effects* on the kidneys and *changes* in hearing, is somewhat disconnected to our conversations with the consultants. Damage to hearing and kidneys isn't like a temporary bruise, slowly turning colour from fresh red, to blue and, finally, yellowish before dissipating completely with the skin returning to a normal, steady state. With cisplatin, the harm tends to be irreversible.

Kidneys, for example, perform critical functions such as balancing our fluids and filtering the blood for impurities and toxic substances, which partly explains why they tend to take a battering during chemotherapy. They are charged with filtering away at one end, the venom injected at the other end. And therefore, it follows that Millie's kidneys are essential to keep her alive. Permanent damage means life-altering consequences and a material reduction in her quality of life. Curing cancer with chemotherapy means causing actual physical and physiological harm to vital organs. Harm that patients will need to carry with them over the remainder of their lives.

Given its risks, additional precautions are taken before cisplatin can be administered. Firstly, Millie's kidney function will be assessed before and after each cycle of chemotherapy. This non-invasive test consists of injecting a special dye into her bloodstream, taking blood samples at periodic intervals and measuring how efficiently her kidneys eliminate the dye: the tongue-twisting, for me in any case, glomerular filtration rate (GFR). A kidney scan by ultrasound is also required. Millie feels some slight discomfort when the cold gel is applied, but given the number and nature of procedures she was submitted to over the last week, she tolerates it very well. Both tests confirm that the anatomy and function of her kidneys is healthy. And ready for abuse.

A baseline test is also undertaken to establish her hearing. Once again, these are non-intrusive tests and confirm that Millie has some mild high-frequency hearing loss on both sides. Since this is likely to be genetic, we shouldn't concern ourselves about it.

'Unfortunately,' Dr H goes on to say, 'cisplatin is also associated with DNA damage to the ovaries that can cause infertility later in life.' He pauses. This means, of course, that should Millie survive this ordeal, she may not be able to have children of her own[19]. It seems a remote problem now, but it all adds up. The blindness, the damage to her hypothalamus and pituitary gland, possible harm to her hearing and kidneys and the cognitive depletion from proton beam irradiation. All as a result of the cure, not the cancer.

Dr H continues, 'If Millie were a teenage boy, I would just give him a wink and suggest he goes into a room by himself and comes back out with a sample for us to freeze. But for girls it's a lot more difficult.' Vanessa and I are completely unable (or at least we were then, as newbies), to challenge this on my daughter's behalf. This is a matter of needing specialist knowledge in this complex area of fertility, and we do not know what questions to ask. Like whether, for example, Millie could store her eggs or ovarian tissue. Moreover, Dr H infers that this isn't a choice because we need to react quickly to contain the growth of cancerous cells and because of Millie's very young age, with ovaries that are not yet fully developed. We are not given the option to talk to a reproductive endocrinologist and, in fact, I don't even know of their existence. Millie is too young to be involved in the discussion.

I have since been told by GOSH that freezing ovarian tissue, or even an entire ovary for later transplantation can, in rare circumstances, be considered for prepubescent girls. This is, however, still very experimental and the procedure is only undertaken in the hope that techniques for using such tissue will eventually become available. This wasn't suggested to us, and an agreement has yet to be decided on clinical best practice for offering families, in the neutral language of the medical profession, prepubertal fertility preservation.

Seven years on, there remains limited evidence that this would work, as I understand it, with only one reported live birth using ovarian tissue harvested before the onset of puberty[20]. This fertility preservation procedure comes with risks, but compared to brain operations, chemo and radiation therapy, it may have been worth considering. Even if it created some false hope.

To have done something, anything, would have demonstrated our concern and the hospital's consideration that Millie's feelings about her fertility, in the future, were worth it. Maybe it's the trying that counts – if something had been done, Millie could have taken some comfort that all options had been considered.

I am probably wrong, but I regret not pushing harder. In any case, all this is far more complex for Millie because the lack of pituitary messaging caused by the cancer and/or its treatment may be the cause of her future infertility.

Millie is aware of this and we have, on occasions, broached the subject on our walks. Vanessa has often discussed this area of Millie's life, bringing the perspective of a woman and a mother.

While we, as her parents, are anxious about this, Millie remains neutral. Even at fifteen, she is still too young to attach much importance to such grown-up concerns. I didn't particularly want or think about having children until I was in my late twenties and in a steady, meaningful relationship. So, this may not bother her until she reaches an age when her contemporaries are starting families and her condition may restrict her choices.

If she cannot choose to have a biological child of her own, will she mourn our decision? Or will she find acceptance? Will future medical progress overcome the damage to her ovaries and help her to conceive? Will she be able to adopt, and will this prospect be enough to fulfil a desire for offspring? Will she even want children? Not everyone does, and that's fine too. The truth is, I don't know. In this, and many other areas, cancer and its cure generate more questions than they provide answers. We'll have to wait and see.

In my more positive moments, I try and reassure myself that this is another instance where the loss that Vanessa and I feel will be different to what Millie will face. We are saddened for something we have ourselves actively sought to experience and know Millie is not going to experience herself in the same way. But we are, perhaps, discounting the choices that progress in reproductive science may offer Millie in the future. Or her own perspective when she's older. Probably because we don't know any better and because we can only contemplate suffering and disappointment from our own vantage point. I certainly hope that's the case.

Going back to just the P in PIE then, this will cause infertility, permanent kidney damage and long-lasting harm to her hearing with all of their practical, emotional and physiological consequences.

The I in PIE stands for Ifosfamide, another alkylating agent, though this one actually is a mustard gas derivative. Ifosfamide, in combination with cisplatin, also carries the risk of damaging Millie's kidneys. This can then cause a decline in kidney function resulting in potentially serious complications, such as fluid retention leading to swelling, high blood pressure, fluid in the lungs, raised potassium levels which can impair heart function, weakened bones, damage to nervous system and even complete loss of kidney function which would require frequent dialysis and the need for a transplant to have a fighting chance of remaining alive. You get the picture.

Finally, the E in PIE stands for Etoposide, a plant alkaloid. This one doesn't damage major organs but mildly increases the risk of Millie developing blood cancer, leukaemia, later in life.

Clearly, chemotherapy is a corrosive treatment. The side effects are doubly devastating because they come collectively and on top of Millie's vision impairment and hormone deficiencies from the cancer and its treatment.

Chemotherapy also carries with it short-term complications which will not make Millie's life any easier during therapy. Unlike the usually remote and unlikely side effects of most over-the-counter drugs, the by-products of cancer treatment are very real on a paediatric oncological ward. Hair loss. Depletion of white blood cells and platelets. Mouth sores. Diarrhoea. Bruising easily.

Dizziness. Tiredness. Nausea. Vomiting. Skin rashes. Confusion. Ulcers. Millie will have all of these, in isolation or in combination, week in and week out, over the course of her treatment.

*

Millie has now been an inpatient for thirteen days with Vanessa and me permanently at GOSH. Ellie and Luca have been staying at their aunt and grandmother's house but will soon start their school spring term.

We are out of the intensive phase of the first craniotomy and about to enter a slightly more orderly phase of treatment. It is by no means less uncertain, but it seems a good time to regroup to consider how we preserve our collective energy in the medium-term to best support Millie, while providing the right level of comfort to Ellie's and Luca's day-to-day lives and minimising the impact that Millie's cancer will undoubtedly have over the coming months.

This surge in loyalty does not limit itself to how we feel about Millie. Something else happens during that first week. Something unexpected. We realise that love is a reflex in tragic circumstances; Vanessa and I close ranks. And we start loving each other more.

In our most vulnerable moments, in our most desperate hours, in witnessing and enduring our respective suffering, the ineffable force that holds our lives together strengthens considerably. Our relationship has changed over the last seven years, as a result of our daughter's illness. The slow depreciation of romantic love that often colours the first decade of marriage has given way to a different kind of emotional attachment. Millie's illness, and being awake to each other's pain, has changed the bond that holds us together. We have become more tolerant of each other's imperfections, more appreciative that whilst we are together, we are also individuals. Our mutual understanding of the damage left in us has made us more aware of the devastation in the respective gardens of our souls. We have grown more compassionate of each other. And whilst the suffering has taken its toll on us too and how we engage with each other, in ways we don't yet fully understand, we've certainly let each other live more freely, for now, because we've died once already.

During the first fortnight at GOSH, we have spent our days in hospital, next to Millie. Now that the more traumatic, uncertain clinical phase is behind us, we must preserve our energy for an intensive treatment plan that will last at least seven more months. As we contemplate the start of chemotherapy, we organise a support team. Vanessa and I will take turns at the hospital. Vanessa, often with her mother, will spend a couple of days and nights with Millie before I take over for the next two-day shift.

When it isn't our respective turn to be at GOSH, we will take Ellie and Luca to school, cook them meals, play with them and reassure them that whilst Millie's illness is serious, it is also curable. Meanwhile, Mummy and Daddy are fully in control in their home. For our children, order, or the illusion of order, will be preserved and protected.

When chemotherapy starts in a couple of days, Millie will be transferred to Elephant Ward (the oncology ward), up one floor from Koala Ward. She is now stable following her operation, and her eyesight shows some improvement.

She can make out very large black letters written on an A4 sheet of paper if it's held, very still, in front of her. Vanessa will stay with Millie for the next couple of days, and I will go back home to Tunbridge Wells to collect my children from Millie's aunt. We regroup to re-establish some semblance of routine to their lives.

The train journey back from Charing Cross allows me my first moment alone in ten demanding days following Millie's diagnosis. As we gather speed out of the station, the buildings start moving backwards against the still foreground of the carriage window. I listen to the rhythmic and familiar clickety-clack of the wheels rolling over the rail joints. As the scenery slowly changes from dense suburbs to sparser housing developments and then fields, this gentle humming shifts my attention to the private landscapes of my mind. I roam amongst some of the emotions I worked hard to supress over the last week to remain functional for Millie's sake. Slowly, slowly, they start nudging towards the surface.

In this trance-like state, I hear those inner voices we all have. The ones that are detached from our earthly meanders, the ones that watch us and evaluate our behaviour, the ones that consider our successes and failures, the ones that pronounce judgment on our decisions, the ones that ultimately determine if we are deserving of self-worth. Those voices rise and become more audible, jumbled up, then all come together, then slowly become distinguishable, one from the other.

One of those voices is angry at the inequitable inconstancy of the universe for allowing this to happen to a seven-year-old girl. Anger at God, even though I'm firmly atheistic but hoping he exists so that I can beat the shit out of him for letting cancer grow in Millie's head and doing nothing to prevent it.

Part of my anger is my frustration that this had happened to Millie. That I could do nothing to change it, that the random nature of life had led to this. That so many small, insignificant events, had they occurred slightly differently, or at different times, would have led fate in a separate direction.

Vanessa and I could have chosen a different month in which to start trying for a second child, or for our first, which would have impacted on the timing of our second. A different sperm could have fertilised the egg that eventually became Millie, out of the millions and millions normally manufactured when attempting to conceive. I regress all the way back to the time of my own birth and beyond. Of course, if that had happened, I wouldn't be here, but then neither would Millie and her brain cancer. Trivial hypotheticals can be multiplied a million times to come up with equally probable scenarios that would have led to the birth of a different Millie, one whom I would have loved just the same but who would not have developed brain cancer. Who would not have suffered.

I could have been more sensible during the latter parts of my sixth form, passed my Oxbridge examinations and gone to a different university. I certainly wouldn't have met my wife as she was connected to a friend from university. I could have decided to cancel, because of a possible last-minute work commitment, my invitation to the wedding in Malta where Vanessa and I met. Equally, all of this can be argued on Vanessa's side too. A sequence of trivial events required for our lives to cross and for all of the chance happenings that led to the exact moment of conception where the DNA of one gamete randomly combined with the DNA of another, multiplying the right way, again and again, except for one tiny rogue cell that started dividing and eventually led to Millie's malignant cluster inside her brain.

This kind of speculation cherry-picks only those moments that could have changed something bad into something good, or something bad into something neutral, or something bad into something less bad. The opposite is, of course, equally probable. Roads not taken could have led to a worse outcome. The likelihood is that the utility I derived from the options I took, on average, over the course of a lifetime, will end up being no worse and no better than those I rejected.

As well as being frustrated I am frightened for what might happen to Millie. Fearful at the prospect of cytotoxic drugs being injected directly in her bloodstream within the next forty-eight hours, over a period of four months. I am frightened on Millie's behalf because I am not sure how she was feeling about the start of her treatment. The thought of Millie being anxious, in turn, increases my own anxiety. I am scared that chemotherapy might not work and that, soon, I would lose Millie. I feel helpless, worried that I might not be able to hold it together for her, for the rest of my family.

I also feel lonely, sad, mortal. As if cancer had sent me into exile, forced to live away from a life I once had and to which I had no hope of ever returning, casting a permanent shadow over the rest of my time on this planet.

Before picking Luca and Ellie up, I drop my bag and have a quick shower at home. This is the home I left before I knew about Millie's diagnosis, that belonged to another me who wasn't burdened with bone-crushing sadness. On my way out, I stop at Millie's bedroom door, which is ajar, as if the universe is warning me against entering it. I don't know if I want to go in, if I should or what will happen if I do. Not really listening to my cautious inner voice, my hand nudges the door open, and my legs carry me inside.

Soft, narrow beams of sunlight stream between half-drawn curtains. Don't they know they are no longer required? I survey her bed, her toys, the books she was once able to read. My sense of smell, like all my other senses, betrays me and detects her scent, her presence from another dimension. All at once, the inner voices that emerged during my train journey gather, collide and detonate in the very core of my being. They fracture all that is me. My legs can barely hold my weight, and I collapse on her bed.

All of the nights and the dark and the murk from the beginning of time combine and well up from the most profound depths of my heart. Everything I had worked hard to organise, to build and to regulate in my life fade away. Harmony, structure and routine give way to the unknown, to unpredictability, to unexplored territory, to terrifying disorder. For now, my life is noise. Limitless and without boundaries in its iniquity. It is the monster that lurks in the cupboard, the stranger you meet in a dark alleyway, the noises you hear in the night, the darkness of the ocean at dusk, the sudden movement in the bushes.

It is the underworld.

And here, alone, not knowing where I am, not knowing what to do, feeling my world falling apart and enveloped by the ephemeral quality of a life and a daughter I once had, I put my head between my hands and cry.

PART THREE

AUTUMN

THEMES

How siblings cope with a cancer diagnosis. Talking to siblings about cancer. Contemplating the loss of a child. Chemotherapy: the good, the bad and the ugly. Chemo's side effects. The kindness of strangers. Ways to think about the future. The truth about "progression-free survival".

And all the lives we ever lived and the lives to be are
full of trees and changing leaves...

To the Lighthouse
VIRGINIA WOOLF

MY SISTER HAS CANCER

About a year after Millie's initial diagnosis, and about three months after her treatment had ended, one night I found my eldest daughter Ellie sitting up in bed. She was a little under the weather and harbouring nothing more than a common cold but crying uncontrollably.

'What's wrong, baby? Are you okay?' I was still treading gently, aware that twelve difficult months of seeing her sister ill beyond all recognition had taken their toll. I just wasn't sure how, and to what degree, and what I could do to ensure that it wouldn't disrupt her childhood or her adulthood. What would be the consequences of her exposure to something so exceptionally traumatic at such a very young age?

'I'm not feeling well,' she sobbed, then continued, somewhat unsettled, hesitant and agitated. 'Am I going to lose all my hair? Am I going to die?'

I knew Millie's cancer and treatment would affect Ellie and Luca in some way, but I wasn't quite prepared for this. Grief clearly confronts everyone, and everyone confronts grief in different ways. I just wasn't sure what *her way* would be. I was less concerned about Luca who was younger and perhaps less aware of the more sinister aspects of this disease. Ellie, on the other hand, straddled the border between understanding and innocence, not entirely aware of the true meaning of cancer. Cancer changed Millie, especially in those seven initial months of treatment, and Ellie, more than Luca, "lost" the sister she had known all of her life.

Her experience of Millie's cancer would have been unique and certainly different from mine and Vanessa's. It wasn't until Millie started to recover that Vanessa and I even allowed Ellie a few visits, mostly at our local hospital where Millie undertook frequent blood tests to monitor the effect of chemotherapy. We wanted to shelter Ellie from the more severe and vivid experiences we were exposed to, and we might not have got that right.

Firstly, despite being the eldest, Ellie was still very young and would have absorbed less information about cancer and was less involved during Millie's treatment. This lack of real understanding may have made her more insecure about her own future, and Millie's, which may have made her anxious for her sister. The hair incident I described earlier was a clear sign, despite her parents' best efforts to focus on the cure's positive aspects, that she had considered the possibility of Millie's death. And no matter how much we tried to keep to our routine, our own distress and absence may have contributed to Ellie's sense of disruption over seven long months of treatment.

The disruption was, first and foremost, emotional. From a stable and steady life, Ellie's world changed when Millie complained of fuzziness and we took her to London. Ellie wouldn't see her sister again for twenty-one days, aside from the odd phone call, photos and a few video messages, until she came home, having endured an intense initial phase of treatment which included a brain operation and a first chemotherapy cycle. Later, Ellie confided that when Millie left for London with "eye problems", she thought her sister needed glasses. She came back as someone else entirely. *This* sister had a swollen face, was disoriented, tired and confused, nearly blind and bore a scar across the crown of her head.

Ellie's outlook was shaken, and her sister's cancer may have affected her own sense of self. At school, with relatives, with the nurses looking after Millie, with her parents' continuous attention to cancer-related demands, there was a danger that Ellie would increasingly perceive herself as the sister of a child with cancer. She would need to develop her own inner resources to make it through this tough time when Vanessa and I were ill-equipped to help. We lacked knowledge and experience to support Ellie in adjusting to this new situation. But we also had colossal demands as our time and emotional energy were focused on Millie. How could we do anything else?

I was painfully aware of the trade-off this increase in our caregiving role required. I knew these disturbances and our lack of parental attention – or rather a redirecting of it towards just one child – would disrupt our functioning as a family. Now that we were on the brink of starting the first cycle of chemotherapy, Ellie's familiar routines would change. We would have far less time for her or Luca's needs, though I sensed he suffered less because he had Ellie, on whom he would rely much more than before. For a while, it was possible Ellie would have no one in whom she could confide or relate in a meaningful way.

For at least four months, Vanessa and I would divide our time; one parent would be at home while the other was with Millie, holding her hand as cytotoxic drugs were injected into her bloodstream. Every two days we switched so that Ellie and Luca would have one parent at a time for the foreseeable future. This was out of the norm, and rationalising with a nine-year-old who sensed but could not meaningfully or accurately grasp the gravity of the situation wasn't going to be easy.

*

When I gathered my senses and left Millie's room, after coming back from GOSH following her first brain operation, I sat down with Ellie. I knew I would not have all the answers but hoped to have the right sort of conversation. Of all the leaflets and pamphlets and factsheets and charity literature on childhood brain cancer and its related treatment, a children's book proved the single most useful for that discussion. *Mary Had a Brain Tumour*[21] is written for children who have been diagnosed with a brain tumour and also for their siblings.

The plot is simple: Mary is a five-year-old girl who lives with her mum, dad, brother and baby sister. She enjoys all the things little girls enjoy like skipping and running and doing cartwheels. But for a few weeks, Mary has been feeling unwell. Sometimes she has headaches; sometimes she feels a bit sick. After a visit to the hospital, a doctor suggests a scan. A smiling nurse tells her this takes pictures of the inside of her head. After the scan, the smiling doctor tells a smiling Mary's smiling mum and dad that Mary has a lump in her head[22]. The book then describes the typical treatment for a lump in the head: surgery, chemotherapy and radiotherapy, highlighting the more visible and temporary side effects of treatment, like hair loss. Mary recovers sufficiently at the end to enjoy a surprise party, with a special surprise present: a (smiling) kitten. The book does mention that Mary's lump is a brain tumour and a type of cancer. It introduced words and phrases I felt Ellie would need to become familiar with since she would hear them, if not from us, then certainly from others.

It was the start of a new school term, and I was concerned that, as the sister of a child with a cancer diagnosis, Ellie would be treated slightly differently by other parents, teachers and her classmates who might question her about Millie. I wanted her to be confident to address these in her own way so that she might feel more in control.

So, after dinner that evening, together, we sat down on her bed and read *Mary Has a Brain Tumour*. I wish I could say that we were smiling as we flicked through the pages, looking knowingly into each other's eyes about Millie's condition, imagining her speedy recovery and, like Mary, gliding through chemotherapy and sitting peacefully on her hospital bed after her first brain operation. Or that Ellie nodded at appropriate times to acknowledge her successful assimilation of this new vocabulary and terminology. Or that we ended our chat with a purposeful hug, a tacit understanding of the collective effort that would be required to cross the uncertain terrain of cancer treatment.

The reality was different, of course. I don't know why I even thought it could be otherwise. Ellie was a child who was confused and unwilling to focus on gaining a better understanding of this frightening situation. She wanted to read the book and be done with it quickly and then left alone. It was going to take more than a children's book for Ellie to adjust to Millie's cancer and its disruption to our family life.

Vanessa and I were also newbies, steering blind, as we all do in the moments that really matter in life. Ellie's getting used to it would be a process rather than an event, and I couldn't control how my children felt about the situation. As parents we would focus on ensuring that we maintained some sense of a normal daily life and routine for Ellie and Luca. We encouraged opportunities to talk and listen, keen that cancer would not become a taboo subject and clear in our message to them both that we were going to be there to support and bear their respective burdens. They deserved the truth at home as much as Millie did in hospital.

I often wonder how Millie's cancer shaped Ellie's childhood in ways I couldn't really understand at the time. How less time together outside of our home affected Ellie and Luca's sense of family life. How these day-to-day changes would, for Ellie in particular, generate a sense of being excluded or isolated from her parents. But the opposite may be equally possible since we coped and learned together as a family, pulling through. It was, perhaps, a survival lesson in itself. It may have matured them more quickly, strengthening their resolve to make life matter, to persevere in the face of adversity and to focus on the silver linings of the many clouds they would undoubtedly encounter over the course of their own life journeys.

But in our initial efforts to protect Ellie and Luca, we didn't let them visit GOSH. Although it's no excuse, they didn't ask us, not after the first brain operation, not during chemotherapy, not during the second and third brain operation. We weren't concerned because Millie was a resident of, respectively, a paediatric neurosurgical ward and a paediatric oncological ward. The worry was that a visit would have involved seeing children with facial disfigurations, those recovering from severe operations to their heads, those who were white as ghosts, thin as skeletons and missing hair. Since we found it difficult to see these children, we projected our adult discomfort onto what we thought Ellie and Luca might feel on the ward.

Our choice may have been misguided and with hindsight, on balance, we wish we had involved them more during that early phase of treatment. Perhaps visits with Millie, and closer proximity to her illness, might have allowed them a deeper understanding of what was happening to our family. It may also have provided them with more information about what cancer meant, less uncertainty and less worry about something mysterious, something they might have imagined was worse than it was, something they didn't, and couldn't, understand.

We chose assurance over awareness. As I sheltered Ellie from what I felt was the worst of times, keeping her at a distance, while being less available as a father, this may have coloured her perceptions of the disease and its consequences. Moreover, it may have led Ellie to feel isolated and that she needed to cope without our support. It pains me to even think about it. I would certainly do things differently if it happened again, though I hope the opportunity won't present itself anytime soon.

There were few such choices about going back to school where Millie's cancer would affect their lives. Obviously,

I spoke with their headmaster, and while the school was supportive, there was only so much they could do to control the impact of Millie's cancer on Ellie's friendship group. How would Ellie maintain her friendships given her emotional state, her changing experience of the world around her and other children's attitudes?

Did she want her mates to treat her normally? Did she want them to recognise that her life was no longer the same? Did she want them to acknowledge her struggle as she learned to cope with a situation so different from the norm, from her own norm?

Social life aside, how would all of this affect her learning? Would she find it hard to concentrate? Would it have an adverse effect on her academic performance, and if so, over what period of time? Weeks? Months? Years? Just as I cannot evaluate Millie's progress against an alternative version of the universe in which she didn't have cancer, the same is true of Ellie.

Nevertheless, in the short-term at least, school provided Ellie with a welcome escape from being the sister of a child with cancer. It provided her with a day-long refuge, Monday to Friday, and she embraced it. But I fear that she also internalised her anxiety, avoiding negative feelings that she did not understand. She was too young to find a healthy outlet for her combined emotions of anger, confusion, sadness, guilt and shame. Vanessa and I were not experienced enough to guide her in their identification and expression so that she could confront and accept them.

Compounding Ellie's sense of isolation was her sister's dramatically altered appearance and character. Since my daughters had been so close before Millie's cancer, Ellie probably felt others were judging *her* when they looked at her sister. Even now, as a confident, free-spirited, loving, outgoing, theatrically extroverted teenager, Ellie struggles to reconnect with Millie. She remains unable and unwilling to articulate the pain and anxiety she must have suffered. Paradoxically, Millie's cancer and its treatment, which required her parents' intense focus, may have had a greater effect on Ellie's mental health.

It might take patience, but I have little doubt that Ellie, who has endured hardship in childhood and grown old before her time, will become a hugely supportive sister. I am hopeful she will, eventually, reconcile the misfortunes of her youth and accept how well she has coped with them. That she will heal from the fissures that the stress she experienced in childhood has exerted on the landscape of her soul. She will realise these experiences, even if they relate to her sister's cancer, had their merit.

Now at age seventeen, she is already maturing and healing as, little by little, she reveals snippets of the inner workings of her heart; a fleeting chat about Millie at the dinner table or in her bedroom, late in the evening, when we bid each other goodnight. She is beginning to understand the complexities of her childhood memories and that she is not alone in experiencing hardship. While some of her friends may not have lived through similar experiences, she appreciates that many have probably suffered their own private disappointments and traumas.

On occasion, during our walks, we have been caught unaware by the rain. A few tiny droplets at first, quickly followed by the heavy, semi-tropical, autumnal downpours foreboding the fast approaching winter. We paid less attention to the natural world around us, not noticing the different kinds of leaves, or their shapes, and no longer taking in the detail of the undergrowth. We focused only on the rain, spending our physical and emotional resources to quicken our pace to reach the car or the natural shelter deeper in the forest. During her own storm, sadness would turn Ellie inwards. At age nine, she lost – for a period at least – her natural cheerfulness and her brightness as her childhood was no longer free from anxiety. The natural event of Millie's cancer dominated her mind, preventing her from awakening her sensitivities to the world around her.

With Millie's cancer, Ellie's world changed overnight and both girls lost the sister they once had. While Ellie's response to Millie's cancer was completely understandable, it also changed how Millie perceived their relationship.

'It used to be me and Ellie,' she might say when I asked about her sister, as we sat on a picnic bench in Bedgebury, overlooking the lake, resting our legs before tackling the last stretch of the walk. 'Now it's more me and Luca. And *part* of me feels like I have lost *part* of my sister. My brother not so much, but then I guess he was too little when I had cancer,' she would say. The emphasis on *part* is mine. It means an element, a component. Millie's inference, even if not conscious, is that she senses the damage to her relationship with Ellie was not absolute. That like many aspects of human relationships, the quality of her bond with Ellie can still improve. It is not static but, like the gentle waves on the lake, it will experience crests and troughs over the course of her lifetime.

For now, Millie yearns for some affirmation that Ellie appreciates what she, as her younger sister, endured. She values recognition and validation – Ellie's opinion matters to Millie, but Millie's matters less to Ellie than that of her peers.

Eventually, Ellie will figure out with greater clarity much of the content of her own mind. And although the rewards will be worthwhile, this takes time and effort – there is no shortcut to gaining introspection. I am optimistic that, along with Ellie's insight will come a greater willingness to share her musings and her own soul-searching with Millie and me. Those are conversations I very much look forward to.

*

For now, on the brink of Millie's first chemotherapy cycle, we would have to be satisfied with a tentative pass at *Mary Has a Brain Tumour*. We would accept that uncertainty and confusion were going to become normal and that life doesn't always go according to plan; plans can often change, sometimes by choice, sometimes by necessity. That whilst we may fall, we can get back up and start again. That stuff breaks but can often be fixed. That we cannot rage forever at the cosmos against adversity. That many aspects of Millie's disease, whilst very serious, enabled us to remain hopeful for the long-term. That the children understood that Mummy and Daddy were here to stay, to love and to do everything they could to provide stability and comfort.

For now, Ellie's focus was starting school as a slightly different girl. We ended last term as a regular family, but this spring term would be different for us all, most of all for Millie. She now resided in Room 605 in Elephant Ward at GOSH and was about to be injected with many doses of toxic chemicals that aimed to kill fast dividing cells and melt away, over four intensive months, much of the tumorous mass in her head.

It was my turn to stay with Millie at GOSH, relieving Vanessa of her duties after her first shift. I dropped Ellie and Luca at school, drove to the station, parked the car and took the train up to London. In the carriage, on firm ground and travelling steadily to Charing Cross, I had never felt more at sea, burdened by grief, sadness, anger and rage. And yet these brief moments of happiness with Ellie and Luca, away from GOSH for a few days at a time, would become an important release that would allow me slowly to understand that I would move forward again, one day...

How little did my children know how much they'd helped their father during his most challenging period.

As I contemplated a life that didn't care much about us, about Millie, but for which many of us care deeply, our mutual love made me even more determined to see this through, and I was looking forward to being with Millie again.

THE P IN PIE

Elephant Ward is an inpatient paediatric ward located on level six of the Variety Club Building at GOSH. Like many of the hospital wings and units, the building is named after its main benefactor: organisations, foundations or wealthy donors giving to the charitable arm of the hospital.

On this ward, all thirteen child residents have or have recently had cancer. They vary in age from infants to teenagers, undergoing some form, or combination, of chemotherapy, immunotherapy or bone marrow transplant. Already weak as a result of their underlying condition, the treatment itself makes them ill and their immune systems vulnerable.

As I drag myself towards Millie's room 605, I catch glimpses of parents, holding their children's hands, playing with them, reading to them and engaged in actions of tender care. Beneath the grown-ups' calm, I glimpse the raging of the storm. They are my reflection.

It is even more sobering to realise that some of these children will not see the end of the month. Many might not live much past the next few years. Of those who will make it, most will suffer serious, chronic side effects from the chemotherapy; they risk infertility, another cancer, memory and concentration depletion and damage to their heart, kidneys and lungs. I breathe deeply, conjure up my best fake smile and enter the cubicle which will be Millie's "home" over the next week or so. Dr H is there, talking to Vanessa. Millie is sitting up in bed, holding a piece of paper.

As I stand by the door, she says, 'Hi, Daddy,' and smiles. I last saw Millie two days ago but now notice that for the first time in two weeks, her eyes lock onto mine.

'Would you like to see the drawing of a blue butterfly I made for you?' she continues.

There are moments in your life you carry with you until your time is up. The bad ones of course, and we had accumulated quite a few over the last fourteen days. But this moment, on Thursday, 18 April 2013, when Millie slowly started to regain her vision, was going to be one of the good ones. This particular moment took the form of a blue butterfly tentatively drawn by the hand of a little girl whose eyes and hands could finally synchronise once more and sketch for her father a few delicate lines on a white piece of paper.

Millie's eyes had given hints of functional improvements recently. Her pupils had always been reactive to light when tested, as they were on Koala Ward. One was more reactive than the other, but we were always told that such signs were good predictors of greater improvement. This could, however, be slow and progressive. It was unlikely Millie would regain her vision overnight, in the same way she lost it.

To establish the damage to the optic nerve, the doctors prescribed a test to measure the electrical response of the eye's light-sensitive cells. An electroretinogram is not intrusive, just a machine that shoots photons at one end and picks up nerve signals in the brain's visual processing region via electrodes at the other. It would confirm that Millie had irreversible and severe optic nerve damage (forty per cent physiological impairment, or loss, approximately) from a lesion caused by the tumour. However, we learned that there was a difference between the physiology of her optic nerve and its ability to provide good functional vision. You can have optic nerve damage and still see perfectly well, but you may be more at risk of compromise if further damage occurs. This could mean the tumour regrowing in the same area, further pressure from other types of illnesses or other unrelated conditions that might affect the optic nerves.

Moreover, improvements in vision are often accompanied by further improvements. So, Millie beginning to recover her vision some two weeks or so after her operation suggested that it would continue to improve. This was welcome good news after a fortnight of battering even though this slight improvement didn't mean Millie's vision had been completely restored.

Aside from the obvious, this was a relief because it justified the clinicians' decision to operate on Millie. Even though there was seemingly little choice at the time, the emotional cost of her suffering, the heavy risks involved, the damage to her skull, the use of valuable NHS resources and staff, were fair trade for the resulting benefits.

The prospect of Millie becoming permanently blind affected me more than Vanessa and perhaps more than the prospect of failing to eradicate cancer altogether. Contemplating a life in darkness for Millie added an additional layer of complexity to what was likely going to be, if all went well, a challenging journey ahead. Quite naively, I realise now, it seemed to add unfairness to an already deeply unfair situation for Millie.

But good fortune, and GOSH's decision to press ahead with brain surgery, had favoured Millie. Her vision would continue to improve, make slow and steady progress while producing some curious effects. During her first cycles of chemotherapy, she experienced a temporary form of colour blindness, often confusing green and yellow. It took time and patience, but seven years on, her vision is stable, near perfect in one eye and close to perfect in the other. She retains only some mild impairment of her peripheral vision.

*

Dr H is also pleased with the improvement in her vision, but consultants being consultants, his expectations remain cautious. He continues to tell the truth as he believes it to be. We have very quickly learned to take things at face value, and not to anticipate the future, taking each day as it comes. Good news is set against the nature of Millie's longer-term prospects. While her vision is clearly important, she is on Elephant Ward for her first cycle of chemotherapy. We don't know yet if it will be effective, how she will react to it over the next four months, and the degree to which it will cause her permanent damage. Dr H is here to provide guidance and to remind us, and Millie, of the task ahead. Millie knows chemotherapy is strong medicine that will kill the bad cells in her head. She is quite comfortable with the process. Later this morning, after Dr H's visit, we will discuss the more visible side effect such as the hair loss – a conversation I have not been looking forward to.

Millie can only focus for short periods and shortly after my arrival, is napping. Dr H, standing near the entrance to the room, speaks softly to avoid being overheard from the patient's bed.

'The prognosis associated with this tumour has been much improved. Over sixty-five per cent progression-free survival is now reported in children.' He pauses briefly before carrying on. 'Although, of course, this does mean that some children relapse and the chance of cure second time around is greatly reduced. But we don't need to think about that at this stage. Let's focus on this first cycle of chemotherapy for now.'

Progression-free survival is how paediatric oncologists like Dr H define the probability of recovery for a child with cancer. This refers to survival without disease *progression* which is, in part, the probability that the patient will not die from the disease within five years of diagnosis. Survival statistics are often what most parents want to know about when their child is first diagnosed, yet tend to be complex to translate into practice. I am not sure what to make of Millie's sixty-five per cent chance of progression-free survival. Does it mean that there is one chance in three she won't make it at all? Or that she will face a thirty-five per cent chance recurrence of the cancer within the next five years, that must then be re-treated, with a different statistical prognosis? Survival statistics are often based on factors such as the type of cancer, its stage and the patient's age. What I am to make of the accuracy of this predictor without really understanding the basis on which the numerator and denominator have been determined? The message is both "children react differently; everyone's an individual" and at the same time, that statistics are useful in providing a sense of direction and making an informed choice for treatment.

As an estimate for a patient's prognosis, in a very general sense, it might be useful to provide an indication of the likely recovery. Or more specifically, of how effective the treatment has been at eliminating cancer cells whilst keeping the patient alive. But how does it help me, as the father of this patient, get a sense of Millie's chances that she will be alive in a month's time? Or a year's time? Or in five or ten years' time? Of what will happen to Millie in the near and far future? Or indeed what her quality of life will be after treatment should she fall into the successful bucket of probabilities? Much of the sixty-five per cent rests on how responsive Millie's cancerous cells will be to chemotherapy's cocktail of drugs. At the level of the individual, it is either effective or ineffective. So that's zero per cent or a hundred per cent. Dead or alive. And if alive, at what cost? Much of Millie's future will depend on how she reacts over the next two courses of the cycle which will indicate whether this particular cocktail was effective. Two months will determine the duration of her future life or the manner and timing of her early departure.

Despite these possible outcomes, oncological wards at GOSH are unexpectedly serene environments from the outside. At a cellular level, chemotherapy wreaks havoc on the body. But in contrast to Koala Ward's palpable sense of shock and crisis, every action in oncology adheres to a specific programme with its own explicit rules and precise plans. It's called a chemotherapy protocol for a reason.

Millie's was PIE, a mixture of three drugs, which are, as you may recall from part two, cisplatin (P-latinum), ifosfamide and etoposide, given over a certain period in specific doses. In the case of Millie's secreting germ cell tumour, the protocol was going to consist of four courses over four months. During each course, lasting approximately a week, the nurses would concurrently infuse cisplatin over a five-day period, ifosfamide over a five-day period and etoposide over a three-day period.

This treatment was the result of cumulative research and the recommendations of a seminal international working group's 1977 clinical trial for intracranial secreting germ cell tumours, established to study treatments for Millie's specific type of cancer.[23] Up until then, the survival rate ranged from ten per cent in the '70s, rising to approximately fifty per cent by the late '80s. Despite this improvement, German and Italian scientists realised that survival prognosis for intracranial germ cell tumours fell behind the rates for other germ cell tumours, so they decided to do something about it[24].

Millie's daily schedule would involve continuous intravenous administration of those three chemicals, through her Hickman line, one after the other, according to very specific timetables and dosages tailored to her height and weight. To make up a protocol dose, the oncologists measured how much of "her" there was and varied its proportions accordingly. Because children undergoing chemotherapy are often underweight, this amount is often calculated according to their body surface area (so in m^2), a more accurate measure of what their size should be given her age.

Chemotherapy is slow, with several one-litre bags of toxic liquids delivered, by gravity and a small pump, into Millie, drop by drop.

A nurse arrives in the morning with the first bag of drug, wearing gloves and a mask because of its toxicity. My daughter's name and hospital number are clearly labelled on its side. The bag is placed on one of two hooks on the IV drip stands on either side of Millie's bed. Before connecting it to Millie's bungs (the plug-like plastic cap at the end of her own line), the nurse follows a strict cleaning schedule to minimise the risk of contamination. This is, after all, an oncological ward where patients whose immune systems have been compromised by their treatments are susceptible to viral and bacterial infections.

Once Millie's line is cleaned and flushed to ensure it's functional, the bungs are thoroughly disinfected and only then attached to the drip. Gravity slowly pushes contents of the container down the drip chamber, below which an infusion pump, a small box, regulates the speed at which the liquid is infused into Millie's veins. It also alerts the nurses (or sleeping parents) when the bag is empty.

This little ceremony is repeated daily for each dose of chemotherapy. The combination of cisplatin and ifosfamide is so toxic to the bladder and kidneys that it requires "hyperhydration" to flush it out and support treatment during the administration of those two agents. So, Millie must be infused with another fluid, day and night, exposed to risks such as electrolyte imbalance and compounding her recently diagnosed diabetes insipidus. The tumour has damaged Millie's ability to produce and store vasopressin, a natural hormone which regulates bodily fluids. This explains why she was constantly thirsty before her diagnosis and the condition which neither her paediatrician nor the specialist endocrinologist were able to diagnose. Millie now takes desmopressin (DDAVP), three pills a day, to regulate her fluid balance artificially[25].

This medication, which enables Millie to regulate her fluids, requires that her liquid levels must be measured frequently, and her sodium level at least three times a day, so the dose of DDAVP can be adjusted. This adds complexity to the management of chemotherapy.

It means keeping track of how much she drinks of water and other liquids such as juices and herbal teas. Vanessa and I chart her intake, all day, every day, with the nurses tallying up the liquids going in. This number is added to the chemicals Millie infuses which is recorded for the doctors and consultants. To measure the liquid coming out, we are provided with greyish disposal bed pans made from what looks like recycled pulp. After Millie has urinated into them, the output is measured and the weight recorded; it's all a little undignified.

This liquid, water, diabetes insipidus and chemotherapy means a lot of wet sheets to change and a lot of sick bowls (made from the same pulpy stuff as the bed pans). The nurses are accustomed to this and put everyone at ease, especially Millie. Nothing is too much, and all of them are clearly happy to engage with Millie throughout their shift. Their skill comes from experience, a natural ability to empathise and from having lived our story a hundredfold, with other parents and children enduring this harshest of treatments.

Despite the nurses' positivity, expertise and helpful disposition, life on the oncology ward is hard, its pace slow and tedious, its emotional intensity crippling. Time ticks by at the pace of drops falling into the drip chamber of the IV stand, with each infusion taking three or four hours to drain. Each little bead of venom is a packet of time that inches its way towards the entrance of Millie's line. Drip… drip… drip… these interminable hours deplete Millie's energy, damaging tissue both healthy and cancerous. Barely recovered from her first brain operation, chemotherapy adds to her fatigue and lack of concentration.

Hooked up to chemo, even her very limited activities when she barely perceives a few photons of light, last only minutes. She can't read; TV images move too fast for her; she is too weak and still too blind to enjoy games in the ward's playroom. She needs the toilet often as litres of medication are continuously pumped into her bloodstream and probably because it takes a while to get the dose of desmopressin right. Everything is made awkward by the one or even two IV stands she needs wherever she goes.

Nights are easier for Millie, who mostly sleeps, but worse for her parents. The nurses' frequent visits to check on Millie or change her bags of liquids, as well as the basic bed and the noise of the monitors, keep us awake. And night is when unbearable thoughts catch us unaware, welling up from deep inside to overwhelm our hearts and remind us how little control we have of the human beings we care most deeply about. It is the casual drift of events, unconcerned about the nature or utility of our lives, or those of our loved ones, that shape our most significant moments.

In this moment, life feels like a Sisyphean myth and chemotherapy the giant boulder we continuously roll up the mountain, only to see it tumble back down at the end of each day. And then, every morning, the following day, we will have to find the energy to heave it up again. Unlike the myth, however, this isn't futile or meaningless as we hold onto hope through the senselessness. The present for us is becoming the most important time of all. We have to learn to live with the hardship and Millie's suffering because we know it could lead back to happiness again.

The suffering of Vanessa and my suffering does not matter. Millie's well-being, her comfort and our need to ease her pain during this traumatic time, that's what matters.

And morning does come, as it always does, even on an oncological ward.

HAIR LOSS AND
FAST DIVIDING CELLS

The metronomic, slow, daily routine of administering treatment on the outside is not mirrored on the inside. Chemotherapy is "cytotoxic". It kills cells. It's easy to get side-tracked by biology's impersonal language. Chemo doesn't just kill cells. Those cells belong to a person. And in our case, that person was our daughter.

In its devastating effects, chemotherapy targets, in particular, fast replicating cells. Cancer cells, clearly, but also those associated with healthy tissues where cells are constantly growing and dividing such as hair, bone marrow – which produces blood cells of the red and white variety – and cells on the lining of the digestive system. All this has well-known side effects on cancer patients.

Firstly, hair loss. It doesn't fall out straight away. Millie's hair didn't start shedding until about a week or so after the end of her first cycle of chemotherapy. And it doesn't all fall at once. It falls in clumps, over a few days. On the pillow, or the sink, or the brush, or the bath drain.

Hair loss is, clinically, entirely cosmetic and probably the least damaging effect of chemotherapy. Hair does grow back a couple of months after treatment finishes. Darker and curlier at first – something which baffled Millie for a while – and then slowly, slowly regaining the texture, thickness and feel of hair pre-cancer. Understandably, this is cold comfort to Millie and she isn't thrilled with the news when we eventually tell her, the day before she starts treatment.

It is upsetting for her on several levels. First of all, she will look different. At seven years of age, Millie is aware of this difference. While she does not remember much about chemotherapy generally, she does recollect losing her hair and even now, she is able to accurately articulate the distress she felt at the time:

'I kept thinking "why me?". Why is this happening to me and not someone else? And why don't I have a choice in the type of treatment? Why can't it be a treatment where hair doesn't fall off?'

As grown-ups, we know this type of questioning is often self-defeating. The universe does not care about agency in the context of our lives. We are often just a collection of random accidents that shape and mould the quality of our existence. Starting with birth. Or the parents we are born to or where and when in the world we materialise in the first place. It's not a choice we make. We have no control over when it will happen. It just happens to us. Much like paediatric cancer. Children are more literal in their interpretation of things. Children need cause and effect to make sense of the world. And all of us, not just young ones, overvalue the negative aspects of our experience against the average utility of a life lived. We tend to remember negative or traumatic experiences more vividly than positive ones, even if the bad ones tend to be, on average, far more infrequent.

And so, I have no answer for Millie on this. Other than to continue to reassure her that this is temporary. That we can find different solutions to make sure her sense of self-worth, which has already taken a battering in the past fortnight, is not further depleted by also now having to go bald for six months or so.

She can now, at fifteen, more lucidly articulate the sense of anxiety she felt at the time. 'Hair is really important when you're a girl, Daddy. And not having any hair makes you different to other children. I was worried about how my friends were going to react to me. I was worried about being bullied.'

And it wasn't just the hair on her head – by the end of the second cycle, Millie lost most of her eyebrows and eyelashes too. A naked ape, if ever there was one, with less fur on her body than the day she was born.

For us, her hair loss was, more than anything else, the tangible external manifestation of the cancer growing within[26]. Up until then, it was all about cell count, nebulous white-grey patches on MRI scans and alphafetoprotein. It felt intangible, impalpable, microscopic in its quality. Millie losing her hair made it more real. More visible at a level we were more accustomed to when experiencing the world around us. We didn't just know she had cancer. We could now see it too. Hair loss was only the start of the metamorphosis into a full-blown cancer patient. Her physical appearance would continue to change and worsen over four trying months of poisonous infusions and medication required to cure her condition.

As far as her hair was concerned, in the end, Millie settled for a practical little Hello Kitty hat, like a temporary plaster for the soul. And it became a talking point every time she met a grown-up, in or out of hospital, a stranger in the lift, another doctor or a nurse or a cleaner or a mum from school. All united in their feeling of compassion for a little girl whose pain was greater than theirs. All blinded by the narrow focus of their empathy, ultimately, though it didn't make me any less grateful for their effort.

'What a gorgeous little hat, young lady,' they would often say, smiling at Millie and making us forget for a brief moment the hardship we were living. Millie's cancer revealed a side to human nature I had seldom encountered during my brief spell in the sun. The kindness of strangers, and yes, cliché police be damned. After years of conditioning about the dangers of strangers, starting with my own parents' warnings, then my teachers, and then in the media, cancer was forcing us to interact with people we knew very little about. But all of them surprised us with a kindness and generosity that even my own family did not begin to match. Or friends. I thought I had many – it turns out that wasn't the case; only one took the time to visit Millie and me in hospital. In the end, none of these strangers revealed themselves to be murderers, paedophiles or rapists in the end.

One such kind human, the managing director of an online travel company, whom we had never met before, heard about Millie through a dad from school. He promptly offered us five plane tickets to Oklahoma City and back where Millie was due to undertake proton beam radiotherapy later on in her treatment.

Another lovely human, a seventy-something resident of Oklahoma City who was unconnected to us, planned a three-month trip so that we could stay at her house while Millie was undergoing treatment.

Or indeed a local private school and its director of admissions and headmaster, who welcomed all three of my children during the three months or so we spent in the city. No entry examinations required, no eleven-plus, no asinine interviews, no senseless emphasis on maths and English. Just kindness, compassion, love and humanity. These are just three examples amongst many others I could have listed.

These ordinary, kind human beings made an extraordinary difference. Paediatric cancer, more than anything else I have experienced, draws out the best in people. Strangers pull together instinctively and ask for nothing in return when cancer strikes a seven-year-old. And whilst empathy – always short-sighted in its quality – may have misdirected their altruistic motives, being on the receiving end of such empathy caused me to reflect on how, when all this was behind me, I might change my own behaviour. How I might measure the value I was contributing to the lives of other humans and the values I might pass on to my own children. How I should continue to temper my ambition for them, as I have always done, academically at least, so they would do well for their own sake, rather than mine. And not to make unreasonable demands of them to become something that was beyond my own capabilities when I was their age. Such insights, however, were useless to Millie during chemotherapy when, already depleted by cancer, her self-esteem was further eroded as she began to lose her hair.

The second set of fast dividing cells suffering collateral damage were those lining the digestive system from the mouth to the other end. On top of the general feeling of nausea, Millie had to endure frequent mouth sores, stomach aches and, depending on the week and the whim of chemical agents, diarrhoea or constipation. Over the first two months of treatment, Millie would lose eight kilos, a third of her body weight. Hospital food was not to blame as Vanessa and I prepared her meals at GOSH, always with fresh organic produce, always from scratch. One exception was Carluccio's home-made *pasta funghi* takeaways Millie would often request but seldom finish. The weight loss was almost inevitable as the body breaks down energy stores to "fight" disease, a process known as catabolism.

And finally, and perhaps the better-known civilian casualty of the cellular kind when administering chemotherapy, the third major group of fast dividing cells affected by these medical toxins are blood cells. Although the treatment is mostly associated with depletion of white blood cells, those responsible for helping the body fight infections, chemo causes low cell counts across all three types, including red blood cells and platelets.

Red blood cells carry oxygen, and, with a low count, Millie would frequently become anaemic, which caused her to tire quickly, or she felt dizzy or would lose the energetic sparkle that often inhabit regular children at play. Equally, her platelets, which help with blood clotting, would suffer, and so we had to be careful with cuts and wounds.

GOSH monitored her blood cell count religiously while undertaking treatment and at home in-between cycles. This is normally managed through a "shared care" programme where the local hospital deploys mobile nurses to take blood at home, or Millie could provide a sample at the local hospital's paediatric unit. For every week in hospital, we would spend three weeks at home waiting for Millie's body and cell count to recover. It was not unusual to be called by her medical team during the recovery phase to take Millie to the local hospital for a blood transfusion when her red blood cell count or platelet count was low. No matter when, no matter what we were doing, we dropped everything, and we went. Blood and platelet transfusions were required almost always at the end of each chemotherapy cycle whilst she was still at GOSH.

For white blood cells, no such prompt ready-made refills were available. Daily injections of Granulocyte-colony stimulating factor (G-CSF) are normally prescribed after a couple of cycles to encourage and accelerate the growth of granulocytes, a category of white blood cells, and stem cells. White blood cell counts would otherwise take cumulatively longer to recover after each cycle of chemotherapy. Although this ensures treatment can continue at pace, it wasn't fun for Millie to have an injection every day for a week after the second, third and fourth cycle of chemotherapy.

The medics explained, in no uncertain terms, that Millie's white blood count would go down substantially when the first cycle of chemotherapy was completed. A normal level is a number greater than a thousand which refers to the number of cells counted per specific sample of blood, usually measured in mm^3. Below two hundred represents a very real risk of infections overwhelming the body and would normally require hospital treatment. Millie's count would go down to *zero* at the end of each chemotherapy cycle and for a couple of weeks afterwards. And so, we learned yet another new word: neutropenia, an abnormally low concentration of neutrophils, a type of white blood cell that makes up the majority of the body's circulating white blood cells. After each chemotherapy cycle, Millie would become neutropenic, leaving her with zero immunity against viruses and bacterial infections for two weeks out of every four, a period when we took extra precautions. We would later discover that chemotherapy was likely to wipe out her active immunity built over her lifetime. So, after cancer treatment, she would need boosters for both artificial immunity, from vaccines against the likes of measles, mumps, rubella, but also to rebuild her defences against other viruses like chickenpox, where immunity was acquired naturally.

Spikes in temperature, or indeed common viral infections causing temperatures of 38c or above[27], were common during treatment, so Millie needed hospital admission for precautionary IV antibiotics. Those visits lasted anywhere from two to four days as an inpatient. At least five or six times during the chemotherapy phase, she would need this treatment, including the day after she came home from her very first hospital admission for her first brain operation and chemotherapy cycle. That one was particularly tough. Millie had been so looking forward to coming home after the most gruelling twenty-one days of her life, followed by the three days we spent gaining her discharge from a large NHS hospital.

The hospital wasn't reluctant to set us free, but Millie's chemotherapy, an already complex treatment, was further complicated by her diabetes insipidus. The damage to a very specialised region of Millie's brain, her pituitary gland and hypothalamus, meant she couldn't regulate fluid retention, though she could judge and respond to thirst. When she was allowed free access to fluid, she could self-regulate but needed daily medication to balance a reasonable level of fluid intake and corresponding throughput. She took, three times a day now, a magical substance called desmopressin. For her, monitoring electrolytes and fluids during chemotherapy, and the need to "hyperhydrate" to reduce kidney toxicity of two agents in particular, ifosfamide and cisplatin – but more so cisplatin – required careful management. Millie's body could not respond appropriately by itself to changes in liquid intake. Desmopressin is an artificial hormone eliminated by the body differently to its natural cousin, vasopressin. Too much of it can lead to an overdose, causing headaches, confusion and drowsiness.

This need for more attention to how chemotherapy was administered, while ensuring the right measure of desmopressin throughout a twenty-four-hour period, extended Millie's hospital stay. This was certainly the case for the first and second cycle of chemotherapy. Less so for the third and fourth where cisplatin was replaced by another similar agent called carboplatin. On average, Millie ended up staying for eight or nine days instead of five, which may not sound like much, but when we felt so helpless and vulnerable, even this extra couple of days was disproportionately difficult and came at significant emotional costs.

And yet cancer doesn't stop to rest. There's no interval, no break, no sabbatical one can take to recharge one's batteries for the next leg of the journey. Treatment must continue at almost any cost. The cost to us as parents was secondary, mattering less than the cost to Millie. And so it should be, though I have often felt responsible for her suffering because I was the one who imposed this life on her. Her condition was as a direct result of being alive and without any decisions made on her part that would have promoted this particular random occurrence. In electing to bring Millie into the world, when Vanessa and I were trying for a second child, I crystallised this accidental outcome that would taint her existence. This sense of responsibility may only last until such time as she has more autonomy and more agency in how she goes about her life. I'm not sure. It often occurs to me that people think more carefully about whether to get tattoos, because of their inherent permanence, than they do about having children. A decision altogether significantly more permanent and more consequential – emotionally and financially – to the fabric of their lives in the long-term than body art. No doubt the shadows which have followed me since the time of her diagnosis have been partly cast by my guilt, remorse perhaps, about the naïve motives which led me to bring another human onto this planet: as a future antidote for my own regrets or to give my life a greater sense of purpose than I had managed to achieve when I was on my own. A feeling which, I fear, will only expire when I, eventually, do.

As sorry as I was feeling about Millie's suffering, I found oncology wards to be one of the great levellers of the human condition. Being there focused my mind on the only problems that really matter: how we love and how we die and in particular, how we contemplate the death of our loved ones and what possible long-term outcomes this particular disease and treatment will yield for the ward's youthful residents. We are all broadly ignorant of how our children's cancerous cellular structures will eventually react to chemotherapy, what side effects they will cause and whether these children will live long enough to justify their hardship.

Millie's cancer taught me something else I had never fully appreciated: to have humility, gratitude and to accept with grace the choices and options available to us and not to spend too much time worrying about the difference between the life I was experiencing and the one I wished for.

Gratitude because after only a few weeks spent on the ward, I began to feel almost thankful that Millie's diagnosis was *only* that of a malignant brain tumour. It wasn't, for example, the stage four neuroblastoma[28] that was tormenting Millie's neighbour, a four-year-old girl, on her first stay on Elephant Ward. This delightful little princess had been a resident for approximately ten months when Millie was first admitted. She would spend a further four years in and out of hospital. Half her life. Her neuroblastoma had started in her adrenal gland, as it often does, and had gone undetected until it ruptured through into her abdomen and into her bone marrow. Her first operation removed a lump the size of a small pumpkin. She underwent more than seventy further operations under general anaesthetic over four years, was subjected to various cycles of chemotherapy, bone marrow transplants, immunotherapy, radiotherapy and other clinical trials. Nothing worked. On the few occasions remission was achieved, her cancer returned and got the better of her eventually. Throughout her titanic struggle and immense suffering, she rarely stopped smiling.

It wasn't a particularly aggressive type of glioma growing in the brain stem of a five-year-old boy across the corridor from Millie. By virtue of its position in his brain, his tumour was essentially incurable and would eventually shut down every bodily system, including his heartbeat, his breathing and swallowing, but sparing his cognitive functions. A cruel way to go. He was being assessed for a potential trial he may or may not have had access to and that would, in any case, have bought him only a little more time. He was receiving radiotherapy treatment, used palliatively to help his symptoms, shrink the tumour and reduce swelling to ease his last days.

Humility because in the face of the greatest adversity, the parents of these children behaved with a dignity and acceptance I could not begin to fathom.

Their composure, their acceptance, reinforced my own experience and recalibrated my outlook. Sometimes, what at first appears immensely threatening can be overcome by the collective combination of medicine and science and love. The hopelessness of their story provided a better insight and perspective into my distress, which I had been unable, until then, to accurately evaluate. Sometimes, it takes others to point out the nature of your own anxiety and how best to appease it. Millie had a curable cancer.

Harder to evaluate was: how curable? How much of Millie's essence and personality would the cure leave her with and for how long? These were the tough questions to answer.

The cure's success, or otherwise, was going to depend on the efficacy of the chemotherapy drugs and the degree to which it could reduce the size of her tumour. This was something normally measured by counting tumour markers specific to her cancer and whether they were going to decline over her first two cycles of treatment. They were substances first measured on diagnosis called alphafetoprotein (AFP) and human chorionic gonadotropin (hCG). The aim was to return these to normal and achieve, midway through treatment, what the medics call "remission", the temporary abatement of cancer. That much we knew.

WILL CANCER COME BACK?

One of the gentler trails in Bedgebury is now gathering autumn's delicate layers of multicoloured leaves. A kaleidoscopic cloak of amber, red and yellow covers much of the forest floor, extending across the mild slopes of Dallimore Valley towards its lakes. Nature is dying, or rather preparing itself to replace the old with the new. Falling leaves suggest the hope of resurgence, in a perpetual cycle that so often plays out, unnoticed, during our spell in the sun.

It's been more than six years since Millie ended her cancer therapy. She has been in complete remission since midway through her treatment, following acute kidney failure during her second chemotherapy cycle.

'Do you think my bad cells will ever grow back, Daddy?' she asks without seeming overly concerned. Like most of her questions, she levels it in a very matter-of-fact, "did you see that documentary on TV last night?" kind of way.

Her anxiety about possible recurrence clearly doesn't match mine. For me, the long-term risks associated with her cancer and its treatment will forever loom large in my mind like a merciless executioner ready to chop away once more at the dignity and hope of a life not yet fully lived.

I think of an appropriate answer, trying to keep a light tone.

'Did you know, Millie,' I say, pointing at the trees readying themselves for three months of dormancy, 'that those trees are made up of ninety-nine per cent dead cells? Only the leaves, buds and root tips, and a thin layer of cells under the bark, are actually alive.' She looks a little perplexed.

I continue. 'When the leaves fall and die, less than one per cent of the tree remains alive. And it falls asleep from the end of autumn and much of winter. When days start getting longer, more sunlight triggers the buds to break and start growing again.

'It was a little bit like your lump at the end of the second cycle of chemotherapy. It was ninety-nine per cent dead, but the doctors continued treatment to make sure there were no live cancer cells left to grow. That's what's really important when curing cancer, and in your case, it is now very, very unlikely that your cancer will come back because none of those bad cells were left in your brain. Even if one of them had been left, by now, six years later, it would have grown enough to be seen on a scan or detected by a blood test.'

The truth is slightly more complicated, but I don't feel Millie is quite ready to absorb the subtle complexities of progression-free survival. When cancer treatment finished, and we contemplated the collective carnage of the disease and its cure, my biggest fear was undoubtedly whether malignant cells were going to start growing back. At some point. Perhaps not immediately, but in the first year, two years, five years, ten years following our return from Oklahoma City.

When Millie was first diagnosed, she was given a two in three chance of a "cure". It's a questionable word, never used in the context of paediatric oncology, where the phrase of choice is "progression-free survival" when referring to a child with cancer's probability of being alive five years post-diagnosis. So "cure" means in a very literal sense not dying within five years from the disease or its treatment, or more accurately, the cancer not reappearing. Life is prolonged but without any certainty for how long.

"Progression-free" means the disease is in remission so its symptoms, that are being treated, are reduced. If they are so reduced that they disappear, the holy grail is achieved: complete remission. Some people confuse this with a "cure", perhaps because of the media, politicians and the charitable sector's use of sensationalist, emotive and even irresponsible language.

Here are a few examples. The Brain Tumour Charity, a UK-based charity engaged in funding research into brain tumours has the following mission statement: "A cure can't wait". Note the singular "a" for cure, and the inference of "cancer" of the brain as a single general disease. Both are oversimplifications of astronomical proportions. Both, deliberately or otherwise, deeply, hugely misleading about the nature and character of this disease. There will never be just one cure, and there isn't just one cancer.

The mission statement of another UK-based charity, the Brain Tumour Research Charity, also focused on research and lobbying for better cure, is "Together we will find a cure". Within its own Annual Report 2018–2019[29], the Brain Tumour Charity's own chief executive officer's message includes (emphasis mine) "we're not going to stop until our vision – a world where brain tumours are *defeated* – has become a reality. We're determined to pick up the pace of progress and find *a cure*". Cancer Research UK's vision is "to bring forward the day when all cancers are cured"[30]. At his State of the Union address back in 2016, even President Obama – or his speech-writer – was seduced by the powerful pull of this particular sound bite, stating, 'Let's make America the country that cures cancer.'

The language of oncology, and of brain tumours in particular, is more precise and depicts a more dignified, truthful representation of treatment. In a hospital, the objective is for cancer or a tumour to be placed in remission. There is an inherent quality to this cancer vocabulary that reminds patients the aim is always to lay aside malignancies, to prolong life, rather than to eliminate death. For a while, a year, two years, five years but never to eradicate completely the possibility of malignant cells regrowing.

Cancer can never be cured like, say, a bacterial infection can be cured with antibiotics. It isn't just one disease; it is many. Complex, multifaceted and ultimately genetic in nature, less a disease and more a common biological transition from a normal cell to a dysfunctional cell[31]. It is driven by changes to a cell's coded instructions for living and replicating, its DNA, as well as factors, amongst many, like too much sun(burn), obesity and smoking. These cause mutations, which cause abnormal and uncontrolled cell growth which form tumours, invade surrounding tissues and send cancerous cells traveling throughout the body, forming secondary tumours. The possibility of cancer lies dormant in all of us. It is the defective by-product of being constructed by millions and millions of replicating cells, so in that sense, it can never be *cured*.

It would be healthier to reframe what "success" means in the context of its treatment by focusing more on the prolonging of a patient's good quality of life. It would be more worthwhile to minimise the negative impacts of cancer, and its treatment, on a life, rather than its total elimination and its potential for fatality *at any cost*. The media, charities and politicians do not make a scientific argument for curing cancer. They promise freedom from the whims and vagaries of circumstance and chance. A promise we know well, as a species, since it is the same assurance all religions since the beginning of time have offered the credulous. It's a seductive language which is hard but necessary to resist.

"Cure" is also misleading because survivors of childhood brain tumours, malignant or otherwise, need constant therapy, which is certainly Millie's case. Cancer treatment ends, but its side effects require management, often over a lifetime. Millie's therapeutic support will never end because of the damage caused by cancer and its "cure".

And while Millie's chances of dying, like other survivors, may eventually reach a level that may not impact her day-to-day existence, or how she contemplates her future, her risk of dying prematurely is higher compared with the average population in the developed world[32]. It is a risk from cancer and from the tumour's damage to her pituitary which, in turn, create hormone deficiencies which can lead to chronic morbidities.

Even after they have achieved complete remission, survivors of childhood brain cancer are some thirteen times more likely to check out earlier than they should. The risks are even greater for those who have only partial remission since their cancer can be managed and contained but never eradicated. So, what do the statistics reveal about the life chances for these survivors?

A hypothetical will help illustrate this: let's take a sample of a hundred children, who, for the purposes of this exercise, are all aged ten and diagnosed with brain cancer. According to a 2010 study[33], five-year survival rates for these children exceed seventy-five per cent[34]. Of course, seventy-five per cent is an average across all central nervous system malignancies, the vast majority of brain cancers, and survival statistics at the level of the individual vary according to their stage and type of cancer. Millie, for example, was given a sixty-five per cent progression-free survival rate based on hers. So more than an even chance but less than the overall seventy-five per cent.

Broadly, seventy-five per cent means twenty-five of our sample of a hundred children, on average, do not make it past their fifteenth birthday. This will be because their cancer doesn't react to chemotherapy or because their remission is temporary and their second round of treatment in a short space of time is not successful or because of complications during or after major surgery, such as a craniotomy, or the location of the tumour in an inoperable region of the brain.

Out of the seventy-five children who make it progression-free past the fifth year, post-diagnosis, a further eighteen will have died before the next twenty-five years have elapsed. So, fifty-six will celebrate a thirty-fifth birthday, and out of the initial one hundred, forty-four won't have made it. This compares to just under two in a hundred over twenty-five years on average against a control, "healthy" population sample.

The most common cause of death in survivors of childhood brain cancer is recurrence of the same cancer within five years. That's why medics emphasise the importance of completing a treatment protocol and why the "cost" of acute kidney failure during Millie's second chemotherapeutic cycle was a risk worth taking. The alternative is an increased risk of dying further down the line even though acute kidney failure can be fatal and toxic agents can cause irreversible damage to healthy kidneys.

Fifteen of the twenty-five who won't make it past the five-year mark will die of a recurrence. That's sixty per cent. The rest, over time, will succumb to new types of cancers, referred to as *subsequent neoplasms*, a needlessly elaborate word for "new growth" which arise from treatment to eliminate the original cancer. The process of getting rid of the disease has increased Millie's chances of getting something similar later in life. Put another way, cancer treatment is so corrosive that it can increase the possibility of other brain cancers attributable to high dose cranial radiation therapy (or indeed the cumulative damage of radiotherapy, chemotherapy and surgery) to develop.

Such "high" levels of progression-free survival rates are so relatively recent, Millie's cancer was not as curable pre-1997 for example, that they constitute as much as we currently know. These survivors form a pioneering cohort who are living longer than ever before, with little knowledge of what happens after the twenty-five-year mark. While anxiety is often a prerequisite of adulthood, living with the very real possibility that I may have to say goodbye to Millie all too soon, still one in four chances even five years on, is difficult to process.

I have often asked Millie about the risks inherent in her type of cancer and the treatment applied to prolong her life. I choose my words with care so that I won't alarm her about an aspect of her disease that she does not yet fully understand or consumes her existence as it does mine.

She would often put my mind at rest by saying, 'I don't really think about it in that way, Daddy. I know there are a lot of risks in the future, but I don't worry about them. It's part of me, of who I am.'

It reassures me that for her, today is essentially the same as tomorrow. It would be strange if she, as a teenager, reflected daily on death and life expectancy. Even adults are pretty poor at assessing risks and probabilities. We don't worry when we should: about crossing the road, sunbathing or riding bikes without helmets. And worry when we shouldn't: about taking a plane, vaccines or radiation from mobile phone masts.

Children, in that sense, are just as bad at evaluating risks as grown-ups, but they also attribute different weight to risks within the context of their life experience. So, they may be less afraid of death or have a different understanding of it than adults do. This was certainly true for Millie.

Throughout the worst of her illness, though she was much younger then, she never seemed apprehensive that her disease might be fatal. She probably had her own sense of it, and as she matures, and now that the worst is behind her, I wonder if she will seek a broader understanding of its possible latent risks.

It hasn't happened so far.

Moreover, other adult survivors I've spoken with don't seem preoccupied with such thoughts. Maybe they do think about it, or maybe they are consciously or unconsciously seeking to remain positive. Or maybe they seek to deceive others to better deceive themselves which is also a valid coping strategy. Some children and adults cope by ignoring all this. It's complicated and as you can tell: I don't know. Will Millie contemplate with more awareness the higher risks of death she has than the average population when she will have to look at life in a way I have never had to?

Perhaps.

But I sense she will be better equipped than me to cope because she has lived with it. As we consider the death of our loved ones, which is especially difficult when it relates to our children, are we misguided in focusing on our regret that they will have missed out on experiences we have enjoyed? The happiness of joyful moments they won't get to experience, the love for one's own children, the moments of unlived bliss?

Maybe this misses the point, or at least I hope it does. In missing the good stuff of life, the bad won't be experienced either: the sadness of a loved one's death, or a beloved's immense suffering, or the deep disappointments we all experience now and again, or feelings of existential pointlessness. Unlived too will be the tragedies that befall us all at one point or another over the course of a lifespan.

The quality of Millie's life, in other words, will be determined not by when she goes, or by assessing the various probabilities and risks associated with surviving brain cancer, but by focusing on what she does during her lifetime. As a father, I want to ensure that she seizes every opportunity, that she enjoys each moment and that she appreciates the simple gift of navigating her waking hours, for their own sake, during every planetary revolution around the sun. And to do so fully, and with fearless abandon, until time runs out.

The quality of her life then, or more precisely her quality of survival, won't be measured by its length but by its width and depth, by the character of her daily meanders, whatever the destination, wherever chance chooses to take her and however far she walks.

PART FOUR
WINTER

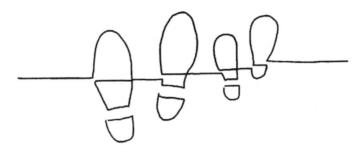

THEMES

Grief. Post-traumatic stress for children and parents. The vocabulary of cancer. Reframing how we think about this disease. Coping with the long-term side effects of cancer. What are they and how can they be managed?

"Have you ever suffered anything similar, then?"
she asked me. "Are you like me? Have you often
drenched your pillow in tears? Are the days of winter
sunshine just as sad for you, too? When it is misty,
in the evenings, and I am out walking by myself, it
seems to me that the rain is falling through my heart
and causing it to crumble into ruins."

"Tu as donc souffert quelque chose de semblable?
me répondit-elle, est-ce que tu es comme moi? Est-ce
que souvent tu as trempé ton oreiller de larmes?
Est-ce que, pour toi, les jours de soleil en hiver sont
aussi tristes? Quand il fait du brouillard, le soir,
et que je marche seule, il me semble que la pluie
traverse mon coeur et le fait tomber en débris."

NOVEMBER
GUSTAVE FLAUBERT

THE SIMPLEST THINGS

The discharge letter following Millie's second cycle of chemotherapy includes the date of admission (7 May 2013) and the date of discharge (19 May 2013). This cycle was meant to last less than a week but grew into twelve long, slow, difficult days. Cisplatin, probably, had caused severe renal failure, from which Millie eventually recovered but only after twenty-four hours in intensive care. She was not the first inpatient to walk the thin line between life and death when chemotherapy is administered.

After just forty-five days since diagnosis, the harsh consequences of cancer treatment were painful to observe. Millie could barely walk[35]. Her vision had, subjectively, improved, but her optic nerves were damaged irreparably, so any improvements were merely functional. And, as a result of her weakened immune system, she had contracted preseptal cellulitis, an infection of the skin and tissues at the front of the eyes. Untreated, this can spread to the brain and cause meningitis. She did recover from that, eventually. She had now, in the spring of 2013, lost most of her hair except for a few scattered little single strands. She was enveloped in "chemo brain", the fog of cognitive impairment and dysfunction that affected her thinking and memory function, generated by the toxic drug cocktail, during and after treatment.

After just forty-five days since diagnosis, Millie is far from the little girl she was before she lost vision overnight. We are deep in the forest, lost in the darkness, unsure if we can ever hope to catch a glimpse of daylight that is Millie's future.

During the initial stages of cancer treatment, and as residents of an oncology ward, hope is cheap. There are the dark nights interrupted now and again by the beeping sound of IV machines to indicate that a particular bag of hydrating fluid is empty and needs replacing. There are perpetual blood tests, and a sodium reading before each and every dose of desmopressin, and the measuring of her every urine sample on a twenty-minute cycle. Every check, every blood pressure test, every drop infused in Millie's body reminds us of our human condition: to suffer and to die.

I feel trapped in a situation which will determine our future and which deprives us of the choice and freedom to run away. I am still not ready to accept the limitations that will inevitably come as a result of Millie's cancer. As evenings descend on Elephant Ward and the nurses turn the lights off, I lie on the small bed for parents, as muffled screams well up from the very depth of my being and explode inside, unable as I am to find a means for their release.

During these long forty-five days in the underworld of cancer, I often begrudge my younger self for feeling emotional discomfort about problems I didn't really have.

Life and cancer are showing me the flip side of the happiness I have not fully appreciated as I have lived it.

We eventually get discharged but not before a platelet transfusion further delayed the temporary reprieve of life between cycles.

*

After a couple of weeks at home, to allow Millie's body to recover from the recent chemotherapy cycle, the phone rang one day after lunch. It was a GOSH number, so I picked it up, called Vanessa and put it on speaker. The previous day, Millie had undertaken her mid-treatment MRI scan and blood test in London. We had been told from the outset that secreting germ cell tumours should show signs of abatement after two cycles of chemotherapy, so the end of her stay at GOSH was significant. These recent tests would confirm whether cancerous cells had been sensitive to the toxic nature of the chemotherapy agents injected into Millie's bloodstream.

If her tumour markers declined, this would mean a reduction in the number of cancerous cells producing those chemicals and improve Millie's chance of progression-free survival. The opposite results would signal the need for a more aggressive strategy; these possible changes in tackling Millie's cancer would likely mean a decline in her chances of survival or more serious impairments later in life.

Dr M was another consultant paediatric oncologist at GOSH and often covered for Dr H when Dr H was on leave or at a conference, as was the case on this occasion. When he introduced himself, I sensed his hesitation. *Probably not a good sign*, I told myself. Today was Tuesday, and the multidisciplinary team looking after Millie met every Tuesday to discuss her case, which meant they had been reviewing her latest scan.

'Following the two courses of chemotherapy, the MRI scan shows a *change* in the tumour.' *Change? Change! Change is never good. He would have been more positive if it were better news.*

'Well… yes… it shows signs of enlargement actually. This is not unusual and probably caused by treatment-induced cysts.' These probably occurred as a malignant cluster melted away and liquid from the chemo filled the space. This was my interpretation of something probably significantly more complex happening as a result of chemotherapy. I thought that was what Dr M was trying to explain.

The team's concern was not so much the enlargement but that additional chemotherapy was unlikely to reduce the size of the tumour's cystic element. 'Given the initial symptoms,' ventured Dr M, 'Millie presented blind because of pressure from the tumour mass, so we feel it is best to operate to reduce the cystic mass sooner rather than later, hmmm… rather than wait until the end of the fourth cycle of chemo.'

This would mean a second brain operation in less than two months. I would quite happily have taken more time on the oncological ward, but before I finished that thought, Dr M added, 'Mr J, Millie's neurosurgeon, has a free slot tomorrow morning. How are you set for coming up later today so we can prep Millie for surgery?'

Despite the shock, the fear of surgery going wrong and its potential for further damage, we must find the courage to contemplate living through the next five to seven days. We know how difficult they will be, for Millie in particular.

First, we must tell her. We try our best to remain composed. We feel it's important not to edit the narrative since she needs to feel some sense of ownership and control about the decision-making process (even though we don't really have any ourselves). She takes it with full composure and maturity, as she has done throughout her treatment and thereafter. Despite her fortitude, I feel the injustice, and this somehow makes it harder, though I'm not sure why. Anyway, there is no time to reflect; Millie packs her bags; Vanessa and I pack ours. We organise for Ellie and Luca to stay at their grandmother's, and we make our way to London. I wonder how closely my feelings match those of prisoners set for the gallows, marching slowly towards some sort of finality. I can barely look at Millie, this packet of innocence, once more on a collision course with fate.

At GOSH, Mr J explains that the operation will be slightly different to the first one. 'We will use the same incision line on her head, but this time, we will access the tumour from above,' he begins.

Mr J is always soft-spoken, deliberate with his words. Always careful to find the right balance between providing factual information, setting objectives, albeit very robust, and expectations. He does not make us feel like he is about to open our daughter's head, rummage inside her brain and extract the whole of the tumour. 'It's still a very complex operation, with serious risks associated with it, but the objective is better defined than the last time we operated,' he says. 'We have a clear plan for a complete resection, subject to what we find and how the boundaries of the tumour appear. It can be hard to distinguish tumour from brain sometimes, so we need to be careful. I'll be chipping away a layer of cells at a time, so to speak.'

These are risks similar to Millie's previous operation: loss of life, stroke and even permanent blindness if the optic nerves are accidentally damaged. Mr J assures that "we will obviously be very careful not to do that" but is reluctant, initially, to provide a percentage to a possible complete loss of vision. After some pushing, however, he advances one in five. Twenty per cent!

It's a risk that is difficult to cope with, even in the circumstances. By now, Millie has regained much of her eyesight and it seems unfathomably unfair that this operation – a second major craniotomy – will have a twenty per cent chance of making her permanently blind. It is the single most difficult element to deal with emotionally during this second craniotomy and, certainly, the most stressful. This is not a one per cent chance of a stroke, or two per cent of waking up with epilepsy, she has a one in five chance of waking up to everlasting night.

I try my best not to appear downhearted for Millie and know this is the right course of action and that, anyway, we have no choice. As I fall asleep in a room on Koala Ward, I prepare myself for the operation, trying to focus on the positives. I trust the level of excellence of this hospital and Mr J's experienced and steady hand.

It bothers me little that this terrifying and unfamiliar situation is causing me emotional harm beyond repair, that every cell in my body will forever remember gazing at Millie, asleep in her bed, innocent to what was about to happen to her. Or that each strand of neuron dedicated to memory will be permanently imprinted with the pain of having to walk her to the operating theatre, of her asking if she could sit on my lap during the process of sending her to sleep, of having to look deep in her eyes and grasp at the last breaths of spirit I have left to see this moment through with composure, for her sake, of squeezing every possible inch of her warm body as anaesthesia takes hold and her eyes roll back. Perhaps forever.

What bothers me most is how Millie will fare later in life after such hardship. Our memories shape us in a very real sense, however subjective the recall. They are part of who we are. In forming what we think we have subjectively experienced, they may well play a direct role in what we believe we are capable of in the future. Will Millie edit her past by erasing unwanted memories and fix new ones? Will she build pieces of fiction, informed predominantly by the stories we have told her over the years about her illness and the way she has conducted herself? Will she recall these events, ultimately just one reality, experienced together but in many different subjective versions – mine, Vanessa's, her siblings, her doctors – as her own distinctive story? Or will the different versions of this narrative slowly smooth out, over time, like water flowing on rock evens out its surface, to become an amalgamated version, a collective gist? A combined memory which may or may not be true in its entirety?

Walking away from the operating theatre, I was clear I did not want this memory to fade. I did not want, in time, to question my reality of what Millie had endured and I went through. My diary from this period aimed to record and preserve our story and its details so that I would always be able to recall what I *experienced* at the time, not as I *remember* it in the present. And, in a sense, so that Millie could read it whenever she could fully grasp its enormity. I was inoculating myself against nostalgia. I needed to make sure I could remember, in the right way, without losing my focus of supporting Millie throughout her treatment and over her lifetime. The more I recorded the miserable intensity of the situation, the better I could achieve this goal. I was also adopting a coping strategy to deal with this trauma. Writing can help and I was neither the first, nor will I be the last, to find solace in processing thoughts in this way. Bach and Mozart composed their operas to air their joy. Master painters painted to express the beauty of life. Writers write to dull their grief, their books often born of pain.

*

Sitting in the café next to the visitors' centre in Bedgebury, sipping a well-deserved latte and overlooking the still, frozen landscape, my conversation with Millie turns to the seasons, and how the lake, with its surrounding plants, looked so different only a few months ago. We try to recall the features of an autumn gone by. It's a good moment to ask questions about her time in hospital, during the treatment phase, to see what she can extract from her memory.

'If I asked you to list what three "bad" things you remember from your treatment, what would they be?' I include a negative bias to the question to see if Millie remembers anything in a gloomy light, anything that might still trouble her about these experiences. Millie takes these kinds of enquiries seriously and thinks for a bit.

'I remember feeling sad when my hair started falling out, after they gave me the strong medicine,' she says with a pragmatism that never ceases to surprise me.

'Then, I remember not liking injections at all. And, in particular, the actual word "injection",' she continues, describing a phobia shared by many survivors.

'And then the third is: I always wonder what it would have been like if my eyes did not get better. If I had stayed blind.'

That's it. This is the extent of her recollection of seven months of brutal treatment. She remembers so little of the things I remember most, and the events I found so traumatic have made so little imprint on her memory. Her recollection differs from mine significantly, and she retains none which has been indelibly tainted by trauma for Vanessa and for me.

The longest, harshest time of my life may well just represent the slightest deposit in my daughter's memory bank. And she is not alone. I have met many other survivors whose recollections are just as patchy. Nature, it seems, finds a way to help these children cope.

When Vanessa and I tell Millie about her cancer, her treatment and the events that have shaped our own thoughts and memories, we are rebuilding what our daughter thinks she has experienced. This strikes me as a positive aspect of the imperfect way memories develop and are retained. By emphasising her resilience, her ability to keep calm, her determination to keep to tasks, to improve a little every day, we may well be reshaping her future capabilities. By reframing her limitations as opportunities for improvement, we hope to help her realise her potential, pay more attention to the present and attribute greater value to the simplest things in life.

REDEFINING CANCER

Approximately six hours after the start of Millie's second brain operation, we receive the best news to date. Dr H has returned from his conference and wants us to review the recent blood test results, taken after the second cycle of chemotherapy. We follow him towards a computer terminal in Koala Ward where he brings up Millie's file.

'Yes, as I thought. Tumour markers have normalised and are down to 2.82. This is a very normal level. I was kind of expecting that.'

This is big! Chemotherapy is working! Millie's beta-hCG, one of the tumour markers relating to her specific type of cancer, has gone from 267, when she was first admitted in April, to within a very normal range at 2.82. It is melting away malignant cells, and the fact that her cancer has been so receptive to treatment is a significant boost to her long-term prognosis. Her progression-free survival, the chance that she won't die anytime soon. It puts her firmly in the sixty-five per cent progression-free survival category and not the thirty-five per cent.

More good news follows nine hours later when Millie finally emerges from the operating theatre. There is no further damage to the optic chiasm, and she has been spared the other life-threatening risks of the craniotomy. Mr J confirms that the operation has gone very well and believes the hypothalamus has not been damaged even though the size of the tumour mass had displaced it.

This hypothalamic damage is an initial concern because it can cause life-altering conditions, including hypothalamic hyperphagia, which causes uncontrollable hunger, rapid and excessive weight gain – not easily treatable – and is exacerbated by a low metabolic rate. The hypothalamus also controls some of our most primitive functions like fight-flight reactions, sleep-wake cycles, growth, pubertal onset, reproduction, milk let-down, thirst, blood pressure and body temperature. It even has a role in behaviour (which can cause ASD/ADHD) and memory.

Mr J's reassurances on Millie's hypothalamus were comforting but, unfortunately, mistaken. In any case, this problem would be addressed later but demonstrated how we must view cancer treatment; for now, all that mattered was that Millie's operation was a success. This was confirmed to us following Millie's post-op MRI scan which, according to Mr J, was an MRI "to frame on a wall". Our discharge letter, which we received when we were back home a week later, also confirmed the "complete macroscopic resection of the tumour". This confirmed that the surgeon's visual opinion matched the post-operative scan.

Despite the clinical success, however, Millie's strength, energy and well-being were at the lowest they had ever been. She was skeleton thin, couldn't keep food down and, after surgery, her temperature spiked for three or four days, probably because her hypothalamus had been disturbed.

She seemed vacant and was totally bald, even missing her eyebrows and eyelashes. She seemed like a creature bereft of hope, lost in the barren, unforgiving, wintery landscape of cancer treatment, somewhere on the other side of sadness.

It required a colossal effort to focus on Millie and to keep our family and working lives going, for her sake. So far, we had coped. We had to hope we would manage to keep on coping. There is no training or class that can prepare you for this.

The third bit of good news, which was all relative because it was linked to Millie's recent acute renal failure, was that Dr H would switch her from cisplatin to carboplatin, a platinum-based agent used in combination with ifosfamide and etoposide. Carboplatin is less corrosive to the kidneys so would not require litres of fluids to flush out, which extended Millie's hospital stay during her first two cycles of chemotherapy.

On balance, in Millie's case, Dr H and the multidisciplinary team at GOSH felt that it was now reasonable to change the "ingredients" that made up the protocol. Millie's tumour markers had normalised; the histopathology of the lump removed during her operation confirmed the tumour, benign or malignant, had been eradicated and she had benefited from a complete resection. Completing the protocol with four courses of chemo, however, was still important. This would minimise long-term risks of recurrence, so the team decided, to use the consultant's language, to "consolidate Millie with a further two courses of chemotherapy prior to localised radiotherapy".

"Consolidate" means giving chemotherapy once remission is achieved in order to sustain it. "Localised radiotherapy" simply means radiotherapy to a specific area of the body, as opposed to, say, craniospinal irradiation delivered to the whole brain and spine with a boost to the tumour areas – as can happen for some central nervous system tumours when they spread. Millie's particular radiotherapy would be "adjuvant", that is given as additional treatment after chemo and surgery, to further reduce the risks of cancer recurring.

I have always had a great affinity with such precise terminology. It may be a hang-up from my auditing days when I was training as a chartered accountant in the early '90s in London. Or growing up with two scientists as parents and being immersed in the day-to-day conversations about baffling chemical reactions I did not understand, like enzymatic synthesis of benzyl chains, catalysed synthesis of peptides, hydrolysis of amino acid derivates and so on. GOSH made no attempt to charge its language with emotion. Something I, and many other parents, valued and found reassuring. Truth, objectivity, balanced judgement are important standards when curing cancer. Parents need to know the truth, and children need to be given the truth in words and concepts that they can understand.

We were living in two separate linguistic spheres. One was the medical, clinical world of GOSH consultants, doctors and nurses which was factual and precise. It reflected the objective way in which treatment was delivered and in which outcomes and possible scenarios were evaluated. The other was outside of GOSH, where the language favoured by laypeople and the media was emotive and often irrational, using vivid metaphorical references to cancer as a "war".

"Your daughter is such a little *fighter*", or "Millie's a winner. She won't let cancer *beat* her" people would say, thinking this would provide me with comfort and pride. It didn't. And it didn't help Millie either. Consider the following headlines, not hard to find, and their depiction of cancer:

BBC presenter Rachael Bland, 40, dies after losing battle with breast cancer[36].

Oncologists dare to talk of a 'cure' in fight against cancer[37].

Brave cancer victim, 28, shares her final photos now she has just days to live only four months after learning she had the devastating disease[38].

Are we winning the War on Cancer?[39].

Cancer, unlike any other illnesses, is something we *battle*, we *fight*, we *lose* to or *win* against; patients are *victims* when they undergo treatments and *survivors* when cancer is cured; we *stand up* to the disease; we are *defiant* against this *enemy*; we *target* tumours with chemotherapy; we deploy *aggressive* treatment.

We don't consider other diseases along these lines. We don't encourage a diabetic to *will* her pancreas to produce more insulin. We don't suggest to an elderly person suffering with arthritis to *command* the inflammation of her joints to reduce. We don't encourage someone with cardiovascular disease to *direct* their heart to perform more efficiently. But we do it with cancer. And worst still, we do it with paediatric cancer. As if this deadly disease could somehow be challenged by Millie's will to resist it. Inferring agency in this way seems stupid at best, cruel at worst.

Our relationship with cancer, ever since my encounter with this disease, has always struck me as gigantically insensitive and ignorant of pharmacology. My role as a father was to protect Millie. To make sure she felt no responsibility to "beat" cancer or to somehow influence her prognosis through the power of thought. Or indeed to feel as if it were her job to combat fast growing cells or that if she behaved in the right way, if she didn't "give up", if she didn't let cancer have the upper hand, she would somehow improve her chances of survival. This is the stuff of science fiction.

While it may seem seductive to think of cancer as something we defeat, there is nothing beautiful about cancer when it can't be cured or when it changes that person irrevocably.

Vanessa and I, however dull it may appear to others, always emphasised the importance of being active: reading, or playing, eating healthily, being compliant with treatment and medicine taking. We felt that how our family spoke about cancer and its treatment was an important aspect of our relationship with it and would influence how we would live its aftermath. We sensed our language would shape Millie's outlook on her illness, how she would tackle her recovery and, in the longer-term, find her place in society. Above all, we wanted to ensure that she never felt personally responsible for treatment decisions or outcomes, or that she could personally influence the death of malignant cells. That she did not perceive this as the last chance to behave valiantly in the face of impending death, as many adults seem to view this disease. As a test of moral character for her or for us as parents. One final opportunity for redemption perhaps. A religious hang-up from a time when we didn't know as much as we do now about the biology of cancer.

History lives on in the language, not always guided by good sense, where cancer patients, or "victims", are "under attack", in a world where cells don't just multiply abnormally, but they are "invasive". We certainly didn't see Millie as a victim, other than, of course, a victim of circumstances.

Such emotive framing is still used by most fundraisers for cancer charities. It's disappointing to see, for example, that the Brain Tumour Charity aims in their 2015–2020 research strategy paper[40] for (my italics) "a world where brain tumours are *defeated*" and to "*fight* brain tumours *on all fronts*". Cancer Research UK's tag line, despite all its wonderful contributions, is, "together we will *beat* cancer"[41].

Given these concerns, early on, Vanessa and I decided to follow the lead of the NHS. Since 2007, with the launch of The Cancer Reform Strategy, the NHS has deliberately avoided the use of "battles" and "wars". I couldn't find a single reference in the 144 pages of the reformed paper[42]. Instead, it used less emotive language, referencing the patient's cancer "journey", with different "pathways" which are adopted depending on the tumour's type and nature.

Millie, and we as parents, prefer this particular framing since it removes agency and rejects the lousy idea that implies that a patient who does not recover from cancer is resigned to die, or lacking will, or a failure.

So, talking to Millie in the language of journeys gave her an opportunity, during and after treatment, to imagine different paths and experiences. We could discuss common destinations, shared goals, her rate at reaching them and how to tackle some of the inevitable bumps along the way. Journeys can have different qualities; they can be emotional, physical, psychological. They can also be hard work, they can be frustrating, lead to dead ends and impasses. They can require sustained daily effort to put one foot after the other along a long road. They might, eventually, yield rewards, and I am confident this will be the case for Millie.

We can only address what it really means to survive cancer and live with its aftermath by reflecting on it with objectivity, integrity and honesty. We should ditch the war metaphors and redefine what success means in dealing with this disease. As parents, we have acknowledged that Millie will never be entirely *cured*, but she can improve her quality of life and her quality of survival by reframing what it means to live with the effects of a disease that took root in her childhood.

We can help with that by choosing appropriate language when we talk to her, in the way we think about cancer and how we support her in accepting the long-term side effects of the disease and its treatment. Only by accepting that she will have to live in harmony with these challenges, and by recognising the shape of her injuries, will she be able to identify the type of bandage required to mend the damage inflicted by this disease.

POSSIBLE FUTURES

The two further cycles of chemotherapy that consolidate her treatment come and go almost without notice. After cisplatin's heavy demands on Millie's body, and kidneys in particular, the switch to carboplatin provides some welcome relief. The treatments last only three or four days, and carboplatin doesn't require the heavy flushing and hyperhydration that so disrupted her fluid and electrolyte balance. In-between the last two cycles, outside of hospital, the chemotherapy's devastating effects continue. When Millie's immunity twice plunges to zero, her white blood cells are boosted with the usual daily injections of granulocyte-colony stimulating factor (G-CSF).

Despite these challenges, her eyesight continues improving and, from a functional perspective, she regains full vision. Her optic nerves, however, remain permanently impaired (she has some sixty per cent left), and any future damage from injury or illness could have serious consequences for her sight

During this second phase of chemotherapy, we learn that she has been accepted for proton beam radiation instead of conventional X-ray radiation. Back in 2013, when Millie was undergoing treatment, her specific type of cancer was not on the indication list for NHS funding, but GOSH and Millie's radiation oncologist, Dr C, felt there was a case to be made to an independent NHS panel. A case was made and was ultimately successful. Even though there are now proton beam centres in Manchester and London, at the time, the only available treatment was outside the UK, so Millie's was undertaken in the US.

Radiation remains an essential component in what the medical profession refers to as "the management of central nervous systems" tumours. Like chemotherapy, however, it comes with associated risks of permanent adverse effects and when the radiation is targeted directly at the head, for "head" read "brain". The switch to proton beam radiotherapy, as opposed to conventional X-ray, is thought to limit the side effects of direct irradiation to this delicate structure[43][44][45]. It's all to do with the difference in the stuff that irradiates the brain. While X-rays are photons with both an entry and an exit dose, because protons are hydrogen atoms with their one electron removed, they follow a different life cycle and have different physical properties. There is a lower entry dose, leading to the proton's maximum dose being delivered in the very specific site of the tumour[46] where the energy is fully released and explodes before dying off. Since it leaves no exit dose, it spares more of the brain matter.

The possible side effects of irradiation to the brain include a lowering of cognitive abilities such as processing speed, length of attention span, a reduced ability to make decisions and an impaired working memory. But there is also potential damage to brain tissue associated with hormonal functions, and exposure to radiation also increases future chances of stroke, second meningioma tumours, and "cerebrovascular sequelae". It is comforting to know that Millie will receive the latest available treatment – treatment which has not changed substantially since then. Although, it would be fair to say here that evidence of absence of harm is not yet conclusive. This is a complex area of comparative research, and much more needs to be done to really understand how to make better direct comparisons between different data points associated with proton as opposed to photon radiation.

Despite having access to the latest technology, after five months of intense therapy, we are still juggling the needs of two healthy children, our work and Millie's demanding schedule at GOSH. The prospect of uprooting our family for at least two months to receive proton beam radiation in America is a little overwhelming. It's not just the distance but also being away from the protective, watchful environment that GOSH has provided from the start. While it has been very tough on everyone, and Millie in particular, we have been cared for in the most professional way. They have reassured us through their positive application of treatment and constant monitoring through blood tests and MRI scans. We have been in a place that knows exactly how to engage with this particularly rare brain tumour disease which has helped us regain some control over our lives.

We had received confirmation from the Proton Beam Centre in Oklahoma City shortly after her fourth chemotherapy cycle and a third brain operation. Before formalising our travel plans, Millie needed a final MRI scan for the centre in Oklahoma so that they could begin planning her thirty or so daily sessions.

Unfortunately, the scan confirmed that Millie had an "enhancing lesion in the left lateral ventricular wall near the callosum". Although the GOSH multidisciplinary team thought this lesion was unlikely to represent tumorous growth, the centre required definite confirmation since it was pointless to irradiate Millie's brain if she wasn't in remission.

This meant a third brain operation confirming that it was a residue of a lubricant that had not been cleaned out entirely during the second craniotomy. This procedure was mercifully much shorter and carried none of the risks of the first two such as permanent loss of vision. Maybe we were becoming "old hands" by then; I can appreciate how parents get sucked into the treatment journey and feel diminishing levels of anxiety when contemplating second and third rounds of chemotherapy. These are often difficult for the children, adding suffering to patients with little prospect of long-term benefit and diminishing rates of success.

*

Travelling overseas with Millie, who, after four months of chemotherapy and three brain operations, still required several medications taken several times a day, was a daunting prospect. But we had decided that all five of us were going to accompany Millie, something I have touched upon in part three. Travelling as a family required more logistical effort and planning but was one of our better decisions at the time. Experiencing this together reinforced our love for each other. It gave Ellie and Luca a more meaningful role: that of being supportive to

Millie as an older sister and a younger brother. Moreover, Oklahoma allowed us to share once more glimpses of the more regular life that lay ahead. One important aspect of our family life was the children. Over the three months there, all attended school together, a place which was filled with the best of human nature. I will always remain grateful to its staff and to its community for the overwhelming kindness and flexibility they allowed us.

The relatively gentle nature of radiotherapy which produced almost non-existent short-term side effects, other than fatigue, also allowed Millie to recover from five very intense months of treatment. Her hair started to grow back, nothing more than a thin, fuzzy layer at first but visibly uniform and Sinead O'Connor-like by the time we left. Hair aside, she was now a different child who slept often during the day, fatigued very easily, couldn't walk far without needing to rest in the pushchair lent to us by friends with younger children. We had disposed of ours long ago.

Millie's brain cancer has been a watershed for our family. We will, for the foreseeable future, always think of life as a before and after April 2013. And Millie has forever been changed as result of her underlying condition and its many, enduring side effects. Oklahoma, with its gentle Indian summer, and the non-intrusive, painless nature of proton beam radiotherapy, allowed our souls time to recover from the most heart-wrenching time of our lives. And we took stock on what the possible long-term repercussions of cancer and its treatment might be.

*

I speak with Millie about the future, on a particularly cold winter morning, as we exhale visible condensation like little clouds of words that gather heat before escaping the narrow confines of our minds. She takes a rather philosophical approach to the limitations that this illness and its therapy have imposed upon her.

'I don't see challenges, Daddy,' she says. 'I see flowers ready to blossom in my mind. When I can't do something, I visualise having to water the flowers with my effort for them to bloom and open into beautiful, colourful plants. I know some of them won't open, but I'm hopeful many of them will. And what's important to me is that I feel I can try and water them, that I can try to make things better, to change things, even if sometimes it doesn't work. That's okay.'

She sees only the roses while I remain acutely aware of the thorns. Is a difference of perspective really all there is to it? A different angle from which to contemplate the landscape or the road ahead?

Maybe it is our perception as outsiders that childhood survivors of brain tumours and brain cancers run a greater risk from the treatment and the disease itself, of impoverished life outcomes. They often rate their level of happiness and life satisfaction higher than doctors and parents rate them. This seems like further evidence of how growing children adapt and their resilience is something from which we should take strength and learn.

Nevertheless, curing cancer remains a dangerous, toxic and corrosive enterprise. The intensity of the therapy and the application of multimode treatments that combine surgery to the brain with chemotherapy and radiation therapy, leaves scars: life-long neurocognitive, endocrine, behavioural and emotional[47]. The cold neutrality of the medical terminology cloaks the very real hardships many survivors face every day. *Neurocognitive, endocrine, behavioural* and *emotional* weaknesses affect, inevitably, these young lives.

For Millie, there are practical consequences, now and in her future. At the start of April 2013, Millie had been a very ordinary, healthy girl, but brain cancer and seven months of treatment forced upon her a different way of living. Then, and now, she adapts as best she can. If we unpack each of the nebulous medical words mentioned above within the context of Millie's life, we can see the disabilities she must navigate.

Let's start with neurocognitive functions.

Brain cancer treatment can reduce the survivor's ability to think, to make decisions, to concentrate, to learn, to process and retain information. For Millie, the combination of three operations, chemotherapy and radiotherapy has had noticeable adverse effects on all these "thinking" functions.

Her working memory, where she stores short-term information, will never recover. This type of memory, for example, is crucial to learning, how to reason and in making decisions. If a simple English language comprehension exercise requires Millie to read and answer questions about a brief passage, she can read and understand the text. But by the time she has turned the page to answer questions about it, she will have forgotten much of its substance. This may seem trivial, but it forms the basis of how we learn almost everything and how we make decisions. Millie, and survivors generally, take longer to assimilate information and keep it in their brain. They need reminders and reinforcement. She can only really focus on one task at a time and finds a classroom filled with conflicting distractions. She struggles to adapt to different teaching styles of different subject teachers. Millie's ability to retain and process abstract thoughts has also been affected.

Since treatment, she has often required one-to-one dedicated help to package information in the right way, to organise her school day, to adopt learning techniques like highlighting, writing things out and constructing mind maps. Shamefully, such techniques aren't universally recognised by doctors or teachers or parents and can cause a child survivor much emotional distress, lead to detentions or even to leave school altogether. More research is needed to understand how to help these children stay in education.

We have been able to support Millie by providing a teacher assistant for three years and more recently, by enrolling her full-time at a special needs school in London. But later in life, these disabilities may make it more difficult for her to find the right job (or vocation), to develop and progress in it, to remain motivated, to manage her salary and other aspects of her life. Millie may well become a vulnerable adult who requires support and protection. How much, and to what degree, is hard to predict at this stage of her development. We just don't know.

Impairments in areas of the brain associated with neurocognitive functions affect the working of the mind. Damage to specialised neurons associated with endocrine functions affect the functioning of the body.

The combined effects of cancer and its treatment (surgery and radiotherapy) have permanently damaged

Millie's pituitary gland and hypothalamus. These small glands are protected by the two sides of the outer brain and located just behind the eyes. Their damage occurs in many childhood survivors of a mid-line, central, benign or malignant tumour. A lot of so-called benign brain tumours (slow growing rather than invasive) take root in the deep, vital and primitive part of the midbrain.

In humans, the hypothalamus is about the size of an almond and difficult to differentiate from neighbouring brain matter on an ordinary MRI. The pituitary gland is even smaller, approximately the size of a pea. Together they make up the hypothalamic-pituitary axis (or HPA) which is the master gland (or "post office") of the main endocrine system. This acts as a hormone messenger system which delivers "letters" in the bloodstream to the body's many glands (or "homes"), which in turn respond and send chemical "letters" back. These glands control many functions, such as growth in puberty, fertility, thirst, hunger, sleep etc that we all take for granted. Not much is known with certainty about how the hypothalamus and pituitary gland interact with each other and with other glands and the degree to which cancer and its therapies impair them. Research is still ongoing in this complicated area, and people with far more knowledge than me understand that these two tiny glands manage most of the hormonal functions crucial for life. They produce these chemical substances directly or by regulating the activity of other hormone-secreting glands throughout the body, such as the thyroid, the adrenals, the ovaries and testes. Millie is therefore on full hormone replacement[48] which involves taking five different types of pills, patches and daily injections at intervals aimed to replicate her natural circadian (day-night) rhythms. This daily regime will continue for the rest of her life.

There are also evening injections for Millie as a consequence of the damage to her pituitary gland. It no longer produces and/or releases growth hormone to stimulate her growth and cell reproduction. This process is essential during adolescence, and it plays other vital roles in the body, such as increasing calcium retention in bones or promoting muscle mass thereafter. Since it is predominantly released into the bloodstream during sleep, Millie must inject an appropriate dose into her thighs shortly before bedtime.

Neither does her pituitary produce nor release an important hormone, the adrenocorticotropic hormone (ACTH), which regulates how we manage stress and fear responses. ACTH stimulates the adrenals to produce cortisol in times of stress, whether you're doing an exam or fighting off an infection. Millie takes replacement hydrocortisone three times a day and must manually adjust her intake when her body needs more. Without the ability to produce cortisol during very stressful times, she faces a serious crisis since threats can reduce sugar levels. The body and brain need sugar to operate adequately so if she were to experience an "adrenal crisis", she would need an immediate glucose and hydrocortisone injection. Just in case this might arise, we carry with us the required emergency kit. Generally, this consists of an injection of 100mg (i.e. a big dose) of hydrocortisone and some glucose.

The pituitary also produces FSH (Follicle Stimulating Hormone) which facilitates the growth of ovarian follicles and is critical during female puberty. Follicles then produce oestrogen and progesterone, which help maintain a regular menstrual cycle. Because Millie lacks FSH, she uses full oestrogen replacement daily patches which deliberately trigger the process of puberty and, to her parents, this feels a little odd.

Another function the pituitary (again!) performs is the release of a thyroid-stimulating hormone essential for a healthy metabolism. Millie lacks this too and takes levothyroxine once a day in the morning.

The hypothalamus controls the release of many of these hormones while producing two very important hormones. One is vasopressin (AVP), which concentrates urine output to avoid dehydration by maintaining an adequate salt and water balance in the body. Before Millie's tumour was diagnosed, it was affecting her ability to retain water which, in turn, caused her excessive thirst and large volumes of daily, dilute urine. To counter this, Millie takes desmopressin (DDAVP), a longer-acting synthetic version of AVP three times a day in pill form.

The hypothalamus also produces oxytocin, a substance still the subject of much research. Well-known for its role during childbirth and milk production, it is increasingly recognised as a powerful neurotransmitter influencing how we bond with our partners and with each other as friends. So, when people hug for example, they show an increase in oxytocin levels.

There is no option to replace oxytocin (that I know of). Science has not yet discovered an effective substitute for what the body produces so well. An inability to produce this hormone may well affect Millie's social interactions, her ability to initiate and maintain healthy relationships. Will a lack of oxytocin flowing in her bloodstream harm her ability to establish friendships, to fall in love, to attribute meaning to the bond she has with her father? Does she care less for her family than she would otherwise? Is she aware of this, and if so, how does it affect her emotionally if her chemical imbalance prevents her from feeling attached to others? It's difficult to evaluate how this might affect her life, but the signs are certainly encouraging to date.

Whilst the hypothalamus produces these last two chemical substances, the pituitary releases them. We don't know if it's damage to the hypothalamus or the pituitary that is responsible for Millie lacking these hormones. It's a problem that we don't know how to fix or even whether fixing it will improve her quality of life. Like everything else to do with this callous disease and its unfortunate side effects, we may never know.

Hormones don't just control the body's physiology; they also influence the way in which we behave.

Relying on synthetic hormone replacement is, of course, not ideal. Millie is prone to fatigue, and, as a result of her neurocognitive deficits, she must work harder and expend more energy on mental tasks than you or I would. Like the Queen of Heart's subjects in Wonderland, Millie must run twice as fast to stay in one place.

The damage to her hypothalamus during her complete resection, her second operation, caused Millie to develop hypothalamic hyperphagia, an excessive hunger, which often leads to obesity. The hypothalamus possesses specialist cells which tell us when we are hungry and when we are sated; these are damaged so that Millie never feels full and is constantly hungry. Combined with a low metabolism, this lends itself to a scenario of continuous weight gain and where diets and increased exercise have little effect.

Although I never really discovered why, GOSH were, at first, reluctant to confirm the diagnosis. Even when we explained to them that Millie was frequently climbing out of bed to eat copious amounts of food. Even when we alerted the team that she was deceitful about her eating, always stealing biscuits and chocolate to eat somewhere undisturbed, and even when her weight rose steadily.

Hypothalamic hyperphagia is a complicated, poorly understood medical condition for which there is no cure. Being overweight is risky as it can lead to several complications for Millie: if she gains excess weight, she will be more prone to Type 2 diabetes, high blood pressure, heart disease, strokes, further cancer, osteoporosis, fatty liver disease and sleep apnoea.

Aside from the serious long-term physical morbidities of obesity, hunger is also an emotional curse as Millie is captive to her appetite. If she does not have food at the right time, hunger takes hold of her entire body and mind, consuming (forgive the pun) her every thought. When she is hungry, she is unable to concentrate on anything else, like her teacher, for example. Distracting herself from food requires effort and burns mental energy that she uses up more quickly than children without her disabilities.

Her hunger is both mental and physical. Her body craves calories because it simply does not know any better and she remains in permanent "starve" mode. Her constant hunger affects her mood and behaviour, which is tightly correlated to her access to food.

Millie has worked hard with Vanessa, a nutritionist, to structure her day and food intake to manage her condition. But it would require another book to detail the practical aspects of the strategies we use to mitigate its effects and maximise her ability to enjoy each day. Or indeed how she will retain control when she is an independent adult – that's where we really need insight. We need to know how to help her "self-regulate" when she becomes an adult survivor, since many find it more difficult. We are hopeful that the "good behaviour" we are guiding Millie towards will put her in good stead to retain some control over her food intake as an adult.

Behaviour is, of course, closely linked to our emotions and the way in which we deal with them.

These functions cover a whole raft of social issues that affect emotional well-being: how Millie engages with others, the degree of independence she might achieve, her future relationships, work, education, psychological functions and her general outlook.

Now that Millie is fifteen, we are beginning to appreciate how she might cope with her emotional life and achieve independence as an adult. Many survivors of childhood cancer do not and find romantic relationships difficult, so they fall back on their families for support. Do these adults perhaps see themselves as less valuable prospective partners? Or do hormonal imbalances, as yet poorly understood, limit their propensity to find comfort in the arms of a loved one? Should they find a partner, many survivors of brain cancer are less likely to have children compared to the general population and even to other survivors of other forms of cancer.

For an adult survivor who has struggled to learn, coped with being bullied at school, as Millie was when she returned from treatment, and had difficulty making friends, finding employment presents yet another challenge. Many survivors must work twice as hard at keeping a job since they suffer from fatigue, have poor vision and hearing, lack mental concentration and social skills. This may lead to financial difficulties; their self-esteem and optimism about the future can fade as they internalise their anxieties and withdraw.

*

I have painted a fairly bleak picture of the many long-term side effects for brain cancer survivors like Millie. And because some seventy-five per cent of childhood brain cancers are now "cured", with many survivors living into old age, I wonder how I should think about their current and future quality of life. As a measure, it depends upon the subjective perspective of an individual survivor. My view and Vanessa's will differ from Millie's; our daughter's experience occurred when she was so young that perhaps she was able to adjust better than her parents.

Quality of life is relative to our current state, as individuals, and to ongoing quality and nature of our respective lives. I know that people adapt to life-changing accidents and diseases in ways they would not have fathomed being capable of when they were first diagnosed. All of us have a tendency to return relatively quickly to a more or less stable level of happiness despite major life-changing negative events. And positive ones too. Winning the lottery has never made anyone permanently happy.

I often contemplate the possible script of Millie's future. If she will be sufficiently happy, with a sense of purpose that makes her life worth living. Research on this matter is positive, with few survivors showing signs of long-term psychological distress from their disease and its treatment[49]. And after seven years rebuilding Millie and her sense of self-worth, I share this hope.

Firstly, I conduct my own time travel by meeting adult survivors of childhood brain cancer in my capacity as trustee of a wonderful charity dedicated to their support[50]. Many of these young people have jobs and careers; they have love in their lives but may also feel sad and face challenges too. They are people just like us, trying to find their place in the world and expect to navigate their way through. They seldom allow their limitations to dictate their lives but try instead to focus on fulfilling their potential. They are well equipped to appreciate what matters, and I am continuously in awe of them.

Secondly, Millie is significantly more optimistic about her future than the one I felt she was capable of enjoying as a result of some of her disabilities. Like all of us, she has good days and bad days, of course, but the ratio is tilting in the right direction. In maturing, she imagines a future filled with possibilities and potential, choices and opportunities.

Even though I exercise caution when asking questions, she will often tell me, 'I don't think about the future in the way you do, Daddy.' She is younger than me and has experienced these events, so her perspective is very different. For example, I ask her, if she could make one of the long-term side effects disappear, which one would it be? She replies without hesitation, 'Probably to feel like exercising more. The food thing isn't a problem for me. I know I can manage it, and I am very proud that I can do it on my own.'

Cancer at a young age has made her more philosophically mature, moving beyond her illness in a very deliberate way. She knows that illness and death can strike at any moment and will, indeed, strike all of us eventually. She does not feel cursed because it has happened to her but better prepared for the suffering, for expecting the unexpected. Perhaps.

But perhaps that's just one consolation from the realm of self-deception. Perhaps when choice eludes us, when we are unable to understand the traumas we experience, cognitive dissonance kicks in.

And the only real thing we're left with is grief.

AN ENDURING LAYER OF COLD

If you turn left at the car park and follow the track just to the right of Bedgebury Visitor Centre, you come to the edge of Marshal's Lake. Millie and I have walked and talked along this trail many times over the past six or seven years, noticing how nature changes its appearance. The lake, and its sister reservoir, a smaller body of water which lies to the north-east, is transformed with the passing of the seasons.

In the spring, with warmer temperatures after the wetter period of the year, the lake water levels begin to rise. Coupled with an influx of nutrients from the surrounding landscape, algae and other vegetation begin to break the lake's smooth surface. The bell-mouth spillway at its uppermost right-hand corner is at its busiest, with vortices of water disappearing into the bowels of the earth, as if forcibly sucked into another dimension. It reminds me of the spring of 2013, when fate decided it was Millie's turn to be exposed to illness of the most catastrophic kind. Every day the rapids of circumstance swept away all aspects of normality, dragging us inexorably towards the darkest, deepest of falls.

As summer follows spring, so the crisis deepened, mimicking the life of the lake. This season brings it warmth, especially to its surface. It is a phenomenon known as stratification, where the warm water at the top is kept separate from the cooler waters at the bottom, speeding up oxygen depletion so that blue-green algae blooms around the lakeshore. Despite the mercurial masterpieces of blossom and trees at their majestic, vibrant best, framed by smooth, blue skies and lit by the brightest of suns, the lake is suffocating. During chemotherapy, Millie's most acute phase of cancer treatment, our life was like the lake in the summer. We were overwhelmed by an environment we could not control while the world around us carried on in its usual ubiquitous disinterest.

Autumn cooling gives the lake a reprieve, as its waters mix again, the vegetation clears and calms its surface. Autumn seems like the season of hope, when nature's decay appears as an interlude to shield itself from winter before its vigorous resurgence in spring. Our two months in Oklahoma were like the lake in autumn when, after the most challenging period of our lives, we dared to look ahead with optimism. Despite a harsh winter ahead, where perseverance and grit would be required to rebuild Millie after cancer treatment, we sensed that life would begin anew. Like the lake, our lives would be rich in potential and new opportunity.

On the lower side of the lakeshore, a memorial bench is empty, its remembered loved ones contemplating eternity. I have rested there a few times with Millie, alone with our thoughts, digesting information shared, thinking of new questions and their possible answers. In the early winter morning stillness, the only sound quivering across the air is the chatter of a rare hawfinch. But you might just hear the subtle crack of slowly shifting ice on the lake's surface as water trapped beneath struggles to break the delicate covalent bonds formed by the simplest of molecules. Most children of school age know it: two hydrogen atoms stuck to a single oxygen one. This exquisite crystalline substance is made up of the same stuff that lies beneath it. Like our lives before and after cancer, water and ice are the same but so different in quality and appearance. We are the same family now as we were then but long for the rigidity of our everyday life to loosen and for our own spring to return.

For now, I will have to wait for this enduring layer of cold, trapped in the deepest depths of my heart, to fade. As I contemplate the lake's smooth surface, the ice within feels like a universal emotion that we must all confront, probably more than once in a lifetime. For me, it formed when Millie was diagnosed with brain cancer, and I realised that her illness and treatment would change her irrevocably. The exact moment when my life became winter came when I carried her down to theatre for her first brain operation on 6 April 2013. I held, for the last time, a child who I would never hold again.

What I felt was grief. My experience of cancer showed me that loss does not necessarily come with the physical death of a loved one. It can mean death of many different kinds.

Grief at the time was compounded by a deep sense of hurt in knowing that Millie was going to suffer during the harshest of treatments. It started with an intense, penetrating and bottomless sadness, a feeling that I couldn't have imagined until then. It suffocated my capacity to look forward. And yet perhaps during the worst of times, sadness serves some purpose, teaching us how to confront the pain.

What surprised me most, during those difficult months, was how Vanessa and I coped with the unthinkable. Everything seemed to happen in slow motion, as if to allow us to adjust to and endure traumatic events. Now I sense that it wasn't fortitude but sadness driving us to focus and turn our attention inwards to the crisis. It required an alignment of all our resources, working together to deal with this major event. Sadness allowed our acute stress response to operate unhindered. The feeling of slow motion wasn't like a lull or an illusion brought about by trauma but our survival mechanism kicking in. It sped us up, enabling us to experience the world at a lower rate of motion and cope better with its change. It gave us more time to adapt.

Although sadness probably has some emotional and practical utility at first, it tends to linger. It doesn't come in stages either, as is often claimed but, for me at least, it has fluctuated like the seasons. At times my life can still be spring, full of promises and potential, or warm and still, like a perfect summer's day. At times it turns to autumn, my days becoming shorter and lacking daylight. Or winter: cold and frozen like the surface of the lake. And so it has been for the last seven years, and so it will continue to be. There are periods when I can only focus on the pain, like the one I feel when I look at photos of Millie pre-cancer. I still find that difficult. These little digital windows in the past reignite the torment, instantly reminding me of life's impermanence and that I will never really get over this particular loss. And yet the hurt, a recognition that grief is work, is all I have left of Millie before her cancer.

The process of healing is time-consuming and requires effort and focus. It brings a greater appreciation for the present, a greater sensitivity to brief spells of happiness and a more acute sense of gratitude as Millie's health improves. The last few years have been the most difficult and heart-wrenching of my life but have provided me with its most meaningful and profound experience.

Millie's age has shielded her from the worst of the despair Vanessa and I have experienced. Our daughter has managed to remain in the simpler, warmer, milder shallows of life. Like many other survivors of childhood brain tumours, and unlike their parents, it is very likely that Millie will not remember her ordeal as a trauma. The challenge for her is life after cancer and learning to live with some of the shortcomings brought about by her illness and, more specifically, its cure, which in itself can bring more life-altering disabilities than cancer itself. There will be limitations to her journey, but we are all actively working to ensure that what isn't possible will not become the story of her life.

Talking to Millie over the last few years has been important for my own recovery. The quiet, drawn-out melancholy that often follows trauma has helped me to supress both hope and anxiety, emotions that have often come together and neither of which is particularly useful. Walking and talking slowed us down. This time made us more aware of modest, gradual improvements in mental and physical health that might have been overlooked if our contemplations had strayed too far off into the unpredictable future.

Focusing on the conversation, and the nature around us, we concentrated on smaller, often milder, problems. And we worried less about the gaps between overly optimistic long-term hopes and probable future outcomes. Irrespective of the season, whether it was the magnolia's red and pink dotting of flowers in the spring, the tall tree canopies of summer, the golden needles of autumn or winter's frosty landscape, nature revealed how slowly the world alters its state. It reminded us to be patient and to take each, small, negligible improvement as a positive and to appreciate the present moment.

Walking with Millie also hinted at another vital aspect of recovery. However special we think we are as human beings, or however much we think we control our own lives, the laws of nature apply as equally to us. Like the trees, the plants and the lakes, we need time and patience for the resolution of things governed by forces immune to our will.

Millie, finally, was the one who encouraged me to keep going, even at my lowest, not just for her sake but for all my children, for the sake of my marriage and my life. By providing insights into her condition, by allowing me to inhabit the more hidden parts of her mind over the last few years, Millie has made me a better father. And I am deeply grateful to her for that.

I hope I have been able to relay my understanding of the deeper issues that arise after a brain cancer diagnosis. There is so much more I could have included about the many long-term side effects of brain cancer and its cure. Challenges and related coping strategies linked to growth, development, puberty, schooling, employment, friendship and love. But I am limited by space and time so will have to leave it for another day – perhaps another book – as we continue our trek along untravelled paths, wherever they may lead us.

We don't know exactly what the future holds for Millie. Or what will happen to her by the end of next year, or in the next five years, or ten, or twenty, or whether she will one day find love, or how her career will play out, or when and how she will one day die. But her disease, and her recovery, with its limitations, hardships and uncertainties, has solidified my faith that, whatever unfolds, she will be just fine. And in being fine, we will remember the consolation of walking and talking as a means to contemplate the journey ahead.

Eight years on from the worst of times, we still walk on the edge of life, but the outlook no longer casts a shadow, threatening to pull us down into an abyss. Instead, we look upwards, hand in hand, our gaze extending towards a much brighter horizon, and we see her future in all its possibilities. We know the road ahead will require hard work, because progress is hard work and often demands change. And that ability to adapt will be key to her improvement. We are confident Millie will discover how best to live, to work with what life has given her, and when she looks back at the end of her journey, she will have a good story to tell.

GLOSSARY OF TERMS

ACTH – Adrenocorticotropic Hormone
ACTH is produced by the pituitary gland and stimulates the adrenals to produce cortisol in times of stress.

Adjuvant
As in "adjuvant chemotherapy" or "adjuvant radiotherapy" – means "in addition to" other types of treatment.

Agents
Chemical substances used to inhibit or slow the proliferation of fast dividing (fast growing) cancerous cells.

Chemotherapy
An aggressive form of chemical drug therapy used to destroy rapidly growing cells (i.e. cancer) in the body.

Cisplatin
Chemotherapy medication, often referred to as an agent, used to treat certain types of cancer.

CNS Tumours
Central Nervous System tumours which include brain
tumours but also any other tumours associated with the
central nervous system (mainly of the brain and the spinal
cord).

Combination Chemotherapy
Using more than one agent at a time to treat cancer.

Craniotomy
A surgical operation in which a bone flap is temporarily
removed from the skull to access the brain. It's a fancy word
for brain surgery.

CSF
Cerebrospinal Fluid: colourless liquid lubricating the brain
and the spinal cord.

Cytology
A branch of medicine specialising in making diagnoses of
diseases by examining samples of tissues (cells) from the
body.

Cytotoxic
Toxic to living cells.

Dexamethasone
A strong type of a class of steroid hormones called
corticosteroids which are used, amongst many other things,
as an anti-inflammatory to reduce swelling from trauma.

Electroretinogram
A test to measure the electrical response of the eye's light-sensitive cells. It is not intrusive: a machine shoots photons at one end and picks up nerve signals in the visual processing region of the brain at the other.

Endocrinologist
A doctor who treats diseases related to problems with hormones.

Etoposide
Chemotherapy medication, often referred to as agent, used to treat certain types of cancer.

G-CSF – Granulocyte-Colony Stimulating Factor
Injections given daily to stimulate and accelerate the growth granulocytes and stem cells after each cycle of chemotherapy (i.e. they help stimulate the growth of white blood cells).

GFR – Glomerular Filtration Rate
Test used to check kidneys' function by injecting a dye into the bloodstream and then measuring, by taking blood at regular intervals, how well the kidneys eliminate it.

Hickman Line
Long, flexible plastic tube inserted underneath the chest wall skin and into the large vein draining into the heart. Used to deliver medication such as chemotherapy or to take blood samples as and when required. More informally referred to as "wigglies" when treating children.

Histology / Histological Appearance
The study of the anatomy of cells (i.e. what they look like, how they are structured), tissues and organs as seen through a microscope.

Hypothalamic Hyperphagia / Obesity
Excessive, uncontrollable hunger leading to weight gain following damage to the hypothalamus.

Ifosfamide
Chemotherapy medication, often referred to as agent, used to treat certain types of cancer.

MRI Scan
Magnetic Resonance Imaging scan is used in radiology to produce detailed images of the inside of the body. Often, a dye is injected to produce better pictures.

Neurocognitive
Relating to the ability to think and reason and make decisions, it includes remembering, processing information, learning, speaking and understanding.

Neurosurgery
Medical specialism concerned with the prevention, diagnosis and surgical treatment of disorders which affect any portion of the nervous system including the brain.

Neutropenia
Having low levels of neutrophils, a type of white blood cell specialising in fighting infection by destroying harmful bacteria and fungi that invade the body.

Oncology / Oncologist
Oncology is the science associated with the study and treatment of tumours. An oncologist is a doctor who treats cancer and provides care for cancer patients.

Ophthalmology / Ophthalmologist
Branch of medicine specialising in eye disorders. An ophthalmologist is a specialist in ophthalmology.

Panhypopituitarism
Condition in which production of pituitary hormones is inadequate or absent as a result of other problems (e.g. damage from brain cancer) that affect the pituitary gland and either reduce or destroy its function or interfere with the hypothalamus.

PIE Protocol
Combination chemotherapy using three agents: cisplatin, ifosfamide and etoposide. Cisplatin is the generic name for the trade name drug Platinol ® – hence the P of PIE.

Platelets
Disc-shaped cell fragments found in the blood whose function is, essentially, to help with clotting.

Progression-Free Survival
Refers to the length of time during and after the treatment of cancer that a patient lives with the disease but it does not get worse.

Protocol
A medical plan setting out the detailed treatments involved in the cure of cancer.

Proton Beam Radiotherapy
A form of radiotherapy that uses protons (hydrogen atoms with their one electron removed) instead of traditional X-rays. The beams cause less damage than traditional X-rays because of the way in which they behave at atomic level and because they can be much more targeted.

Radiotherapy
X-rays or similar forms of radiation used to treat disease, in particular cancer and benign tumours.

Recurrence
When the same cancer returns after a period of remission.

Remission
When the signs and symptoms of cancer have lessened (or, in the case of complete remission, are not detectable). As far as cancer is concerned, remission often correlates with the size of the tumour (if the tumour shrinks, it is said to be in remission).

Resection
Removing, by means of surgical procedures, all or part of a tumour.

Residual
What cancerous cells or other tumour mass remains after attempts to remove it have been made.

Resus / Resuscitation
Intensive care unit in a hospital, where patients are woken up after an operation in a medically controlled environment.

Secreting Germ Cell Tumour
Type of brain tumour called as such because it often secretes a substance called alphafetoprotein (AFP). Some types of germ cell tumours (non-germinomatous) may also secrete a hormone called human chorionic gonadotropin (hCG).

Sequalae
A medical term for late effect or the, often adverse, consequence of doing something or treating something in a particular way.

Tumour Bed
The tissue that surrounds a cancerous tumour and usually provides it with oxygen and nutrients.

Tumour Markers
Usually substances, proteins, more often than not, which present in or are produced by cancer cells in response to cancer. Markers often provide information about a cancer, such as its type or how aggressive it might be.

ENDNOTES

1   Under the auspices of NICE – the National Institute for Health & Care Excellence – a public body of the Department of Health in England, which publishes evidence-based health and care guidelines

2   Under the auspices of RCPCH – the Royal College of Paediatrics and Child Health, – a professional body of paediatricians in England which publishes its own evidence – and consensus – based health and care guidelines for children (eg after a stroke) or endorses those developed by other professional societies (eg the collaborative paediatric oncology, (CCLG) and endocrinology (BSPED) guidelines on rare pituitary and other endocrine tumours; also on Success Life After Cure Ltd website)

3   Previero, M. (2015). Dear Millie – diary of a child with cancer. Matador UK.

4   Slight digression: the word "diabetes" comes from a Latin word broadly spelt the same as the English equivalent. The Latin borrowed the word from the Greeks where diabetes meant an "excessive discharge of urine". "Insipidus" is Latin for tasteless, named in contrast with its unrelated namesake – mellitus, from the Latin for 'sweetened' – referring to how this was initially diagnosed many moons ago: by tasting the urine.

5   Ozawa, M., Brennan, P., Zienius, K., Kurian, K., Hollingworth, W., Weller, D., Hamilton, W., Grant, R. and Ben-Shlomo, Y. (2018). Symptoms in primary care with time to diagnosis of brain tumours. Family Practice, 35(5), pp.551–558.

6   Ansell, P., Johnston, T., Simpson, J., Crouch, S., Roman, E. and Picton, S. (2009). Brain Tumor Signs and Symptoms: Analysis of Primary Health Care Records From the UKCCS. PEDIATRICS, 125(1), pp.112–119.

7   Brain cancers are often referred to as Paediatric Central Nervous System (CNS) tumours or Childhood Brain Tumours (CBT) and I will use the terminology interchangeably from now on.

8   Udaka, YT. and Packer, RJ. (2018). Paediatric Brain Tumours. Neurologic clinics. neurologic.theclinics.com.

9   Cancer Statistics for the UK. (28 Jan 2022). Retrieved from https://www.cancerresearchuk.org/health-professional/cancer-statistics-for-the-uk#heading-Zero

10   Louis, DN., Perry, A. and Reifenberger et al. (2016). The 2016 World Health Organisation Classification of Tumours of the Central Nervous System: a summary. Acta Neuropathology, 131, pp.803–820.

11   Whilst craniopharyngiomas are classified as benign tumours, they are anything but because of their location in the deep midbrain. Attempting to "cure" this type of tumour almost always gives rise to life-altering complications.

12   More specifically, it was a non-germinomatous germ cell tumour, of which there are several subcategories. Hers was a mature teratoma – a type of germ cell tumour made up of several types of tissue and consisting of both benign and malignant cells.

13   Combined detection of AFP (alphafetoprotein) and β-hCG (beta subunit of human chorionic gonadotropin) serums is an essential part in the evaluation and treatment of

nonseminomatous germ cell tumours and in monitoring the response to therapy. Alphafetoprotein (AFP) is the major protein of fetal serum but falls to an undetectable level after birth. The primary malignancies associated with AFP elevations are hepatocellular carcinoma and nonseminomatous germ cell tumours. The beta subunit of human chorionic gonadotropin (β-hCG) is normally produced by the placenta. Elevated β-hCG levels are most commonly associated with pregnancy, germ cell tumours, and gestational trophoblastic disease. Perkins, G., Slater, E., Sanders, G. and Prichard, J. (2018). Serum Tumor Markers. [online] Aafp.org. Available at: https://www.aafp.org/afp/2003/0915/p1075.html.

14 Henley, W. and Howlett, J. (n.d.). Invictus.

15 This was the case when Millie was undergoing treatment back in 2013 – it may be that it is held on a different day now.

16 Armstrong, GT. (2010). Long-term survivors of childhood central nervous system malignancies: the experience of the childhood cancer survivor study. European Journal of Paediatric Neurology, 14, pp.298–303.

17 Consent to medical treatment can be quite complicated and outside the scope of this book. In a very general sense, young people aged sixteen or seventeen are presumed to have sufficient capacity to decide on their own medical treatment, unless there's significant evidence to suggest otherwise. There may be circumstances where children under sixteen consent to their own treatment. The test here is that they should be believed to have enough intelligence, competence and understanding to fully appreciate what's involved in their treatment and the risks associated with possible choices. This is known as being Gillick competent but Millie, aged seven, was far behind this threshold so we, as her parents, had responsibility to consent for her.

18 Chemotherapy agents can also be given by mouth in tablet, capsule or liquid form and have similar benefits and risks as chemotherapy given by infusion. Today, many cancer patients receive oral chemotherapy as a treatment, including some types of brain cancer.

19 I have since been told that the youngest children are also the ones most likely to preserve their fertility compared with adults. So, as ever with cancer and chemo and side effects, it's complicated.

20 McDougall, R., Gillam, L., Delany, C. and Jayasinghe, Y. (2017). Ethics of fertility preservation for prepubertal children: should clinicians offer procedures where efficacy is largely unproven? Journal of Medical Ethics, 44(1), pp.27–31.

21 Children's storybook – Mary has a brain tumour. CLIC Sargent Publications: https://publications.clicsargent.org.uk/ products/mary-has-a-brain-tumour.

22 The book was, as they say, age appropriate. None of us were smiling at the time of Millie's diagnosis.

23 Secreting germ cell tumours of the central nervous system (CNS). First results of the cooperative German/Italian pilot study (CNS sGCT). Available at: https://reference.medscape. com/medline/abstract/.

24 Regrettably, I was only given this particular paper much later in the process from the oncologist in Oklahoma City where Millie would end up receiving proton beam radiotherapy, as the third leg of the treatment for this type of brain cancer. It's a shame, because I know many parents crave medical information often unavailable or too specialist for laymen to identify as relevant. Information provided on GOSH factsheets and the myriad of literature produced by charitable organisations is just too general and unhelpful, too simplistic to be of real value. For another fantastically useful and more recent paper on the subject, one I wish I had been directed to at the time though I won't go into any details about it as part

of this book, do refer to: Abu Arja, M., Bouffet, E., Finlay, J. and AbdelBaki, M. (2019). Critical review of the management of primary central nervous non-germinomatous germ cell tumors. Pediatric Blood & Cancer, 66(6), p.e27658.

25 Millie takes desmopressin for this condition, sold under the trade name DDAVP. It is a man-made form of vasopressin and widely available in the UK. Millie is lucky. Desmopressin was not synthetised until the late '70s, with vasopressin extracted from cadavers instead.

26 This is somewhat misguided because hair loss is actually a sign that fast growing cancer cells are being killed (like fast growing hair cells). It's a sign that cancer is being cured.

27 Actually, protocol's guidance is two readings of 38° or above an hour apart – if that happens, then it's straight to hospital for precautionary IV antibiotics.

28 Neuroblastoma is a type of cancer that forms in certain types of nerve tissue. It most frequently starts from one of the adrenal glands – as it did for this little girl – but can also develop in other parts of the body. Stage four means it had spread to several other organs.

29 Brain Tumour Charity Annual Report 2018–2019: https://assets.thebraintumourcharity.org/live/media/filer_public/25/79/25797ee0-f646-4322-822d-ef598b4db756/annual-report-2018-2019.pdf.

30 https://www.cancerresearchuk.org.

31 I still remember my PE teacher in secondary school describing cancer in its most succinct essence. I was educated in France, and we were talking about cancer and smoking and lung performance etc. He said, in a heavy southern accent of the Languedoc, a coastal region bordering the Mediterranean Sea midway between Spain and Italy, *'le cancer, c'est simple, hein! C'est les cellules qui déconnent.'* Cancer is quite simple, really. It's cells messing about.

32   Arrymstrong, GT, Liu Q, Yasui, Y, et al. (2009). Long-term outcomes among adult survivors of childhood central nervous system malignancies in the Childhood Cancer Survivor Study. J Natl Cancer Inst, 101, pp.946–58.

33   I am not aware of a more up to date one at the time of writing. What follows, therefore, is a hypothetical example based on data which is ten years old, on data points collected over decades prior to the data making it in the 2010 paper. Modern treatment data is as yet unable to project too much into the future. So, some caution is required here in making too much of the 2010 paper in terms of what it might mean in practice for Millie or indeed for other adult survivors of childhood brain tumours/cancer.

34   Armstrong, G. (2010). Long-term survivors of childhood central nervous system malignancies: The experience of the Childhood Cancer Survivor Study. European Journal of Paediatric Neurology, 14(4), pp.298–303.

35   Correspondence from GOSH like discharge letters and clinic follow-ups tend to be positive in their language. This particular discharge letter expresses approval at how "Millie is now able to walk by herself with more confidence"…

36   HELLO! (2018). BBC presenter Rachael Bland, 40, dies after losing battle with breast cancer. [online] HELLO!. Available at: https://www.hellomagazine.com/celebrities/2018090561941/bbc-presenter-rachael-bland-dies-breast-cancer/.

37   Ft.com. (2018). Oncologists dare to talk of a 'cure' in fight against cancer | Financial Times. [online] Available at: https://www.ft.com/content/9a51d044-4a3e-11e8-8c77-ff51caedcde6.

38   Mail Online. (2018). Cancer victim, 28, shares final photos to raise awareness of disease. [online] Available at: https://www.dailymail.co.uk/news/article-5361943/Cancer-victim-28-shares-final-photos-raise-awareness.html.

39 Newsweek. (2018). Are we winning the war on cancer? The good news. [online] Available at: https://www.newsweek.com/are-we-winning-war-cancer-good-news-799096.

40 The Brain Tumour Charity: Assets.thebraintumourcharity.org. [online] Available at: https://assets.thebraintumourcharity.org/live/media/filer_public/00/a3/00a3dd32-903b-4376-b057-20b23d3964d4/research_strategy_rgb_digital_final_online_version.pdf.

41 Cancer Research UK – www.cancerresearchuk.org.

42 Nhs.uk. (2007). NHS England. [online] Available at: https://www.nhs.uk/NHSEngland/NSF/Documents/Cancer%20Reform%20Strategy.pdf.

43 There is, I am told, little proof of this based on available data, a lot of which still requires collecting. Additionally, there are concerns, for example, that because it is more direct and deeper, it may damage vessels (causing more strokes). Moreover, IMRT (Intensity-Modulated Radiotherapy – a more targeted conventional radiotherapy) is already a lot more focused than older radiation regimens people have been comparing it to, so it is still very difficult to compare and against which patients (surgery, no surgery, which types of surgery) etc.

44 Antonini, T., Ris, M., Grosshans, D., Mahajan, A., Okcu, M., Chintagumpala, M., Paulino, A., Child, A., Orobio, J., Stancel, H. and Kahalley, L. (2017). Attention, processing speed, and executive functioning in pediatric brain tumor survivors treated with proton beam radiation therapy. Radiotherapy and Oncology, 124(1), pp.89–97.

45 Carbonara, R., Di Rito, A., Monti, A., Rubini, G. and Sardaro, A. (2019). Proton versus Photon Radiotherapy for Pediatric Central Nervous System Malignancies: A Systematic Review and Meta-Analysis of Dosimetric Comparison Studies. Journal of Oncology, pp.1–17.

46 A phenomenon called the Bragg peak for anyone interested in finding out more about it.

47 Nicklin, E., Velikova, G., Hulme, C., Rodriguez Lopez, R., Glaser, A., Kwok-Williams, M. and Boele, F. (2019). Long-term issues and supportive care needs of adolescent and young adult childhood brain tumour survivors and their caregivers: A systematic review. Psycho-Oncology, 28(3), pp.477–487.

48 A condition known as panhypopituitarism, which means she has inadequate and/or absent production of hormones of the pituitary gland, which in turn interferes with hypothalamic secretions.

49 See Armstrong GT – 2009 above.

50 SUCCESS – Life After Cure Ltd www.successcharity.org.